DANCE WITH ME, DADDY

HIS-STORY OF BUILDING HEALTHY CHURCHES AROUND THE WORLD

ROB CAMPBELL

PRESS

DEDICATION

I *dedicate this book to the following two families: My physical family and my spiritual family.*

First, thanks to the bride of my youth, Susan, for your support, encouragement, and continual interest in this project. Indeed, you are my best friend! I also extend my gratitude to my two daughters, Taylor and Kayley. You didn't stand on the sidelines while Daddy secluded himself in his office pursuing this lifelong dream. Instead, you were eager participants seeking to help me and be with me. Each of you remembers that heart wrenching line from one of our favorite movies. "Doctor, remember– these girls are my life." Most assuredly, you girls are my life.

Next, thanks to my spiritual family, Cypress Creek Church. I cannot imagine a better place to pastor. You have consistently displayed your love, grace, patience, accountability, and encouragement to me. You wholeheartedly embrace God's vision for this church family. God has captured your hearts and He has amazed us all as we have seen the invisible become visible, the dream a reality. May His dance continue in our midst. Specifically, I extend my thanks to CCC's pastoral team (Jim and Debbie, Eddie and Krista, John and Audrey, Kathryn and Walker, Cecilia and Bob, Jennifer, Daren, Grayson, Allison, Chris, Michele and John). Further, thank you Overseers (my comrades at arms)– Bob Belvin, Eddie Blakley, Tracey Dean, Jim Donaldson, John Ellis, Mike McCoy, and Terry McGinnis. You gentlemen have partnered with God in making me a better husband, father, leader, pastor, and friend. Finally, thank you Shepherds of CCC– the soldiers in the trenches being used by God on the front lines of ministry. Your commitment to the vision is awe-inspiring, spurring me to become a better pastoral team leader.

RECOMMENDATIONS

"Rob and I have been close friends and ministry colleagues for more than 20 years. His influence on my life and ministry is immeasurable. In *Dance With Me, Daddy*, you will experience the principles and life stories of a remarkable church, which is led by a truly humble and gifted man. Rob's passion for souls, cells and healthy church life is contagious! Rob's style is engaging and very practical. He indeed is a practitioner of all he writes. *Dance With Me, Daddy* will encourage, challenge and inspire you to settle for nothing less than true relational Christianity."

Pastor Steve Smothers,
Dripping Springs Community Fellowship,
Texas

"Rob has written a profound, but practical book that will change not only our paradigm of church life, but how we pursue a healthy church mentality and lifestyle. I experienced life change when I visited Cypress Creek Church. Further, I experienced the same transforming power as I read the stories in *Dance With Me, Daddy*. I will share and publish this book for the churches of Korea as I know it will have a great impact on all who read the stories of how God changes lives and is bringing health to the church."

Paul Jeong,
President of Natural Church Development and Touch
Korea

"I have had the awesome opportunity of Rob ministering to my church family. The presence of God was strong in our midst. Upon reading **Dance With Me, Daddy**, I had the same strong feeling of God's presence. In this book, Rob is telling very practical stories which center around the eight quality characteristics of a healthy church proposed by Natural Church Development. Rob's wit and bright sense of humor are evident throughout this book. The deep insights he presents will bring great inspiration to anyone who will read this book. I strongly recommend this book to anyone who wants to see God bring health to your church."

**Pastor Young Mo Ryoo,
Hansomang Community Church,
Seoul (South Korea)**

CONTENTS

FOREWORD

Rob has traveled around the world to discover the principles he now records in this extraordinary book, *Dance With Me, Daddy.*

Rob's writing style is winsome and direct. He shoots straight at the heart, helping the reader apply principles that work. He transparently shares His own life, call, and how a church driven by cells can penetrate a city, country, and world for Jesus Christ.

God will touch you deeply—like he did me—as you read miraculous stories taking place at Cypress Creek Church and throughout the world.

Admittedly, I'm not a disengaged reader. I visited Cypress Creek Church in 2002 with a team of hungry pastors. We were amazed at God's work: Junior highers leading weekly "outside the church" cell groups. A prayer ministry you can feel. Encounter retreats that transform lives. A church that is penetrating the world.

Having visited CCC, I can now say that Rob Campbell leads one of the most exciting cell churches in the U.S. Planted from scratch in 1993, CCC numbers over 100 cells and 1000 people in Celebration. Not content with growth in one place, Cypress Creek Church has become a church planting movement.

We left amazed, blessed, and excited to apply the same principles you'll find in this book. Get ready for God to work in your life as you read this book.

Joel Comiskey

INTRODUCTION

"Let them praise his name with dancing!" (Psalm 149:3a)

A re we willing to dance with God? Both of my daughters love to dance to the Lord. Recently, my daughter Kayley, inserted her favorite worship CD into the jambox in our living room and waited for the tunes to begin. I watched her from a relaxed position in my leather recliner. The music began and she turned to me and stated, "Dance with me, Daddy." Now, I confess to being a lousy dancer, but how could I resist this earnest plea from my youngest daughter? I looked around the general area to see if my wife and oldest daughter were in sight. They were not. I didn't totally want to make a fool out of myself. I lifted my body from my chair and began to dance with Kayley. Her radiant smile and steady giggle captured my heart and dismantled my human apprehension. Soon, the living room was transformed into a Worship Center and the whole family joined in.

God, our Daddy, is asking his children, "Will you dance with me?" I am speaking more of a dance of the heart although much can be learned from dances that involve our physical bodies. Indeed, God's word is packed full with dances that are appropriate and biblical. These dances are physical manifestations of God capturing an individual's heart. God is calling his church to a new dance. This dance will present a radiant bride to him in preparation of his return. Let's allow Jesus, the groom, to lead his bride (the church) in this heartfelt dance.

For illustrative purposes, chapters five through eleven begin

Dance With Me, Daddy

---

with an explanation of a specific cultural dance and a heartfelt dance from scripture. The cultural dances were researched and written (with a little help from Dad) by another dancer in my family, my eldest daughter, Taylor. Further, the testimonials that precede these chapters were penned by my fellow dance partners, the pastoral team of Cypress Creek Church.

In the pages that follow, my greatest hope is that you will experience the dancing hand of God that is permeating and penetrating life-giving churches around the globe. Will you join the dance of God?

xiv

PREFACE

Years ago, a four-month-old infant experienced a bizarre death. This young, baby boy bled to death after being bitten by the family's pet rat. The tragic incident occurred in the homeless family's car as they were sleeping in a trailer park one-quarter mile from Disneyland. One local authority stated, "You would think the baby would be crying (from the repeated bites of the pet rat). You would expect the baby cried a great deal. Everybody here is shocked and angry...I have never seen anything like this before. Never, never." What a tragedy! A young life snuffed out due to the insidious behavior of the family's "pet."

Consider your emotions that surface as you read this dire account. Are you angry? Are you filled with sorrow? Do you feel hurt? Can you empathize with this tragedy? Are you sensing your own sense of justice rise within you? Do you want someone to pay for this needless death?

Now, consider God's sorrow. Indeed, God does sorrow for a child he has created who was killed. Can you sense his hurt or pain? How does God's justice and/or mercy play into this scenario?

Another body—a spiritual body—is slowly expiring in America. This body is a portion of God's people, the American church.

In America today:

- All Protestant denominations have declined by 9.5% over the last 10 years [a loss of approximately 4.5 million people while the population has increased by approximately 24.2

million people].
- In the past 50 years evangelicals have failed to gain an additional 2% of the American population.
- Not one county in America has a greater churched population today than it did ten years ago.
- Church attendance has declined by 7% in the past 18 years.
- There exist 195 million unchurched individuals making this country the third largest mission field in the world.[1]
- Islam could be the second largest religion in the country by 2015 through the conversion of university students and those in prison.[2]
- Only 37% of Americans are in a church on any given Sunday morning. Of those who attend a church, only 52% are believers.
- Approximately 4,000 churches close their doors every year.
- 90% of Pastors believe they were inadequately trained to cope with ministry.
- At any given time, 75% of Pastors want to quit.
- 80% of Pastors believe pastoral ministry has affected their families negatively with 33% believing that the ministry is an outright hazard to their family.
- 70% of Pastors do not have someone they consider a close friend.[3]
- Approximately 50-70% of the churches started in America close their doors in less than 5 years.[4]

According to the "2001 Yearbook of American and Canadian Churches," the total U.S. church membership includes over 151 million people in 320,697 various congregations.[5] It would be my assumption that the majority of these church members would agree that Jesus is to be the head of the church. *"...Christ is the head of the church, his body, of which he is the Savior...And he [Christ] is the head of the body, the church; he is the beginning and firstborn among the dead, so that in everything he might have the supremacy" (Ephesians 5:23b, Colossians 1:18).* If Christ is the head of the church, then no one else can be the head. However, the body of Christ (the church) is rapidly declining in this nation. Apparently, a large majority of the churches in America have "head" colds. Slowly, but methodically, Jesus' headship has been replaced by man's ideas and initiatives. Bit by bit the church's position, power, and purpose is being consumed.

Globally, however, one can view a very different picture concerning Christ's body.

In the world today:

- 80,000-100,000 individuals are receiving Christ every day.
- 3,500-4,000 new churches are planted every week.
- The last five years have produced the greatest growth in the church in all of history.[6]
- Evangelical Christianity is the world's fastest growing religious movement with 645 million evangelicals in the world today or 11% of the world's population. This movement is growing 3.5 times faster than the world population. Further, the Pentecostal and Charismatic churches are growing 4.5 times faster than the world population.[7]

A common greeting of one of my friends is, "What gives, man?" I challenge you with the same question, "What gives, man?" Is the American church cursed? Are we too consumed with our own ideas versus God's plan? Has pride led to our decay? Is this just a season of decline? What can we learn from "hot pockets" in the world where God is moving in powerful ways? Why does revival tarry in this land?

I have an honest confession. I do not know the answers to these questions. I do believe, however, that there does exist a template for identifying and understanding the essential qualities for a healthy church. This template can be found in Christian Schwarz's book entitled *Natural Church Development.* In this book, Schwarz presents practical conclusions drawn from the most comprehensive study ever conducted on the causes of church health and growth—more than 1000 churches in 32 countries on six continents took part in this project. To date, 4800 American churches representing over 60 denominations have completed the NCD survey which helps to diagnose the health of a specific church.

Schwarz's extensive and world wide research found that

healthy, growing churches seem to share eight quality characteristics. These characteristics are: Empowering Leadership, Gift-oriented Ministry, Passionate Spirituality, Functional Structures, Inspiring Worship Services, Holistic Small Groups, Need-oriented Evangelism and Loving Relationships. Although Schwarz does comment on church growth, the needed ingredients listed above intensely focus on the health of the church. My contention is that health precedes growth. "Jesus did not have a church-growth ministry. He had a healthy ministry. Jesus' teachings are a prescribed health regimen."[8] Thousands of pastors have tried to build ministries on sick foundations. While you may not agree that these eight quality characteristics represent a conclusive barometer of a church's health, they do provide a good launching pad which should stimulate research and honest contemplation.

The book you are currently reading is a compilation of contemporary stories of how God is moving in various regions in the world. Further, each chapter meshes with the eight quality characteristics that Schwarz has identified. I have labored at putting flesh on the bone of each quality characteristic. The chapters that follow are filled with stories that will grant you a deeper understanding of each quality characteristic. This book has not been written to answer all your questions about church health and growth. Nor has this book been written to postulate new theories of "how you might make your church hum." This book will not present a "quick fix" for your church's current state of affairs. In a nutshell, this book was written to whet your appetite, to salt your oats in your personal and corporate pursuit of God who is always at work around you.

Let's collectively join our hearts in eliminating the pet rats that are dissipating the precious life-blood from the body of Christ in America today.

PART ONE:

HIS STORY AND MINE
"COME DANCE WITH ME"

Chapter One

"The Power of Story"

"Mankind doesn't need art, what he needs is stories."
G.K. Chesterton

This book you are reading is not a complex book. It is a simple book filled with stories meshed with life giving principles. Martin Luther stated, "Christ could have taught in a profound way but wished to deliver his message with the utmost simplicity in order that the common people might understand. Good God, there are sixteen-year-old girls, women, old men, and farmers in church, and they don't understand lofty matters!....Accordingly, he's the best preacher who can teach in a plain, childlike, popular and simple way."[9] As one peruses the gospel accounts, you see that Jesus' life was not an essay. His life's purpose was not to spearhead a systematic theology that might be passed down through the generations. Further, the gospels do not record one long sermon in which Jesus pontificates a philosophy of life. Instead, you discover that Jesus' life was a story. His story has transformed billions of lives and remains the most inspiring, penetrating and awe-inspiring story ever heard.

In his excellent work, *The Silence of Adam*, Larry Crabb reminds us that man, like God, was meant to speak forth stories to display the wonders of God. Crabb writes, "Throughout Genesis and the Old Testament, man is the mediator. He is the connection between the past and the future. He remembers the stories of old, the stories of his fathers and grandfathers. And he lives to transfer the story of God to the next generation, to his children and grandchildren."[10] Genesis 1:27 explains that *"God created man in his own image, in the image of God he created him; male [zakar] and female he created them."* 'Zakar' means "the remembering one." In essence, man is literally named by God to remember and to pass on to future generations his memories. Elie Wiesel wrote, "God made man because he loves stories."

I trust that you know storytellers. They are probably very dear friends to you. As you converse with these individuals, a myriad of stories are meticulously woven through the fabric of your conversation. Typically, sanguine personality types are big storytellers. Storytellers build relationship, cement friendships, and display transparency and vulnerability through the spin of conversation. As you recline on the couches with your friends in your hunting cabin or gather around the table with your family during your annual family reunion, stories will be shared. These vignettes remind us of the past and point us to the future. The swapping of stories fills the pages of God's Word as well. For example, read closely this story of God's mighty work recorded in Nehemiah 9:9-12:

> *You saw the suffering of our forefathers in Egypt; you heard their cry at the Red Sea. You sent miraculous signs and wonders against Pharaoh, against all his officials and all the people of his land, for you knew how arrogantly the Egyptians treated them. You made a name for yourself, which remains to this day. You divided the sea before them, so that they passed through it on dry ground, but you hurled their pursuers into the depths, like a stone into mighty waters. By day you led them with a pillar of cloud, and by night with a pillar of fire to give them light on the way they were to take.*

Habbakuk 3:2 says, *"LORD, I have heard of your fame; I stand in awe of your deeds, O LORD. Renew them in our day, in our time make them known; in wrath remember mercy."*

Psalm 44:1-3 reads,

> *We have heard with our ears, O God; our fathers*
> *have told us what you did in their days, in days long ago.*
> *With your hand you drove out the nations and planted*
> *our fathers; you crushed the peoples and made our*
> *fathers flourish. It was not by their sword that they won*
> *the land, nor did their arm bring them victory; it was*
> *your right hand, your arm, and the light of your face, for*
> *you loved them.*

At the last supper, Jesus stated to his disciples, *"This is my body given for you; do this in remembrance of me" (Luke 22:19).* Do you see "the remembering one," the God-man commanding us to tell his story? Indeed the scriptures are chock-full of stories—God's most effective means of breaking into our hearts and minds. "God is telling a story, a story full of life, love, and grace, a story of hating evil and honoring good, a story rich in drama, poetry, and passion. As we see his story told through our lives, we find the courage to handle the inevitable confusion of life. We find the strength to move ahead, to take risks, to relate deeply, because we are caught up in the larger story of God."[11]

We live in an era in which storytellers hold the key to the future. "The heart, the gift, of storytelling is the exchange of experience and the 'experience of other.' Telling stories builds bridges across generational divides."[12] "Storytelling and other appeals to the imagination are effective with many pre-Christian and post-Christian populations, and a sole reliance on direct propositional speaking is seldom as effective as it should be anywhere."[13] Rarely does a night pass without my daughter asking me, "Daddy, will you read me a story?" Kids love stories. Please be a "remembering one" and realize that God delights in telling His story ("history") through your life. The power of this simple book lies in the stories of how God has worked in the lives of individuals. You will remember these stories.

Enjoy the journey. Be captivated by God's story expressed

through the lives of people around the world. But, don't be content in simply reading stories about God's activity. GET YOUR OWN STORIES of God's marvelous work in your own life and church.

Daniel Taylor encourages by stating, "Here is the story: it starts, 'In the beginning, God created,' and it runs through time and through Biblical history and church history and now up to the present time. And now you come, too. You join the story, you be a character in that story."[14]

But first, let me begin with my story.

Chapter Two

"My Story"

I have been around church folks my entire life. My father was a pastor for twelve years before entering the Army chaplaincy when I was nearly three years old. Being an Army brat, my family bounced around the United States appreciating new surroundings, a multitude of schools and a myriad of ethnic groups. The first eighteen years of my life, I lived in ten different locations including Texas, Missouri, Maryland, Kentucky, New York, Florida and Hawaii. I cherished and fully embraced the adventure, living out the military idiom, "Home is where the Army sends you."

Throughout this nomadic phenomenon, I learned to adapt to new settings, adjoin to new people, forge relationships, and habitually say "Adios" to an ever evolving network of friends. I would not trade these formative years in my life. I learned the challenges of being a minority. I learned how to journey from Staten Island to Manhattan via bus, ferry and subway. I learned how to surf the waves in Haleiva and snorkel the crystal clear waters of Hanauma Bay in Oahu. I learned about survival as a skinny, white boy with glasses in an overcrowded, urban high school.

Further, I experienced many different churches that make up the body of Christ. At the age of nine, I received Christ at Grandview Baptist Church in El Paso, Texas. My father baptized me a few weeks later. I loved my church experience. The church (no matter where my family lived) was the centerpiece of our home.

I was reared by good parents and prevailed in my family of origin in the midst of three older sisters. Yes, I was the only boy and the baby. My dominant childhood emotion was a sense of destiny. Little did I know during the first eighteen years of my life that my destiny would be a church leader. I'm sure my high school buddies in Honolulu raise an eyebrow knowing that today I am a pastor and church planter. You see, as a senior in high school at Hawaii BAPTIST Academy, I cited "pizza and beer" as my favorite meal in the yearbook. I was selected as "class clown" the final two years of my high school career. Spiritually, I was carnal, but present at various church services and functions. As a child and teenager, I recall many good people who loved and encouraged me in these various churches.

After my high school graduation, I journeyed to the university to continue my studies. Literally, thousands of miles separated me from my parents, and I was free. Of course, I did not fully comprehend freedom. As a matter of fact, I fully misconstrued "my" freedom. In a few short months after my arrival at the university, my freedom collided with God's destiny and his call on my life. This adventure intensified when I met a fellow student, Steve Smothers.

Steve radiated Christ. He was fun, good-natured, handsome, well liked, friendly and interested in me. I remember thinking as an eighteen year old, "This guy is cool and he is a Christian. How can this be? Something is up here and it doesn't make a whole lot of sense." He did not come across as a holy nerd. He was not religious or pompous. I spent a fair amount of time trying to figure him out. As I dug deeper into his life (watching with a critical eye and listening with keen ears), I discovered an incredible treasure. Steve was genuine, real—right down to the core of his heart. His life and lifestyle were attractive to me. Certainly, there were other men and women in my life who succinctly fit the characteristics that I admired in Steve, but I was not moved by them. I am not blaming anyone for not successfully entering into my life. I accept full responsibility for avoiding or evading God's people around me. Today I know that God is never early or late; He always arrives at just the perfect time. Steve was a gift from God that I cherish to this very day.

My friendship with Steve grew. We journeyed through our university years seeking God and growing in Him. We had a great time at the university and even studied a few times along the way. I watched his friendship and courtship with Lesa. I was a groomsman in his wedding to Lesa. He watched me bounce around the map of romance. He has known Susan as long as I have known her. Steve and Lesa participated in my wedding as I married Susan. As young couples, we shared countless hours discussing church, children and the future. Everyone needs a Paul, a Timothy and a Barnabas. Steve has been my Paul, my Timothy and my Barnabas.

By 1992, I had accumulated ten years of youth ministry in three different churches in South Central Texas. Each of these churches were incredible gifts to me and my family. God blessed richly during this youth ministry decade of my life. I loved youth ministry and just knew that this is what I would do for many more decades. I did not want to become a senior pastor. Meeting, knowing and discipling youth was a blast. Being the primary leader of a church body appeared boring and bland to me. Then one day, I was apprehended by God.

Before I go into this experience, let me summarize a few bothersome impressions that repeatedly surfaced during my decade of youth ministry. First, I noticed considerable motion and energy in the church, but limited success in reaching not-yet believers. The people of the church were serving—serving themselves! Second, I continually heard people give incredible accolades to the youth ministry of the church, but holistically they maintained benign feelings about church life. In essence, the youth ministry was a church within a church. Numerous adults wanted to serve in youth ministry because they were longing for life.

Next, the people's passion for the Lord was sporadic and frequently undetected. A spark of passion for God generally followed a big event, retreat or "revival" meeting. Ultimately, the passion was short lived, shallow and circumstantial. Further, I realized that the people paid the pastors to keep the church humming. The pastoral staff acted as hirelings. Empowering and equipping people for the work of the ministry was preached, but very seldom was it a reality. A subtle shaping of the pastor took place. This shaping was not from God, but the invention of the people. Pastors retreated to pleasing the people who put bread on their table and money in their pocket.

I repeatedly noticed that most churches were interested in protecting their own interests and fortresses. Competition among churches and area pastors was expected and acceptable. Additionally, stories about how God was moving came from other places on the various continents of the world. I remember thinking on a number of occasions, "Man, I wish God would move in a phenomenal way right here." These powerful, moving stories were distant and ethereal. Finally, I was annoyed at the leadership's unyielding allegiance to denominational initiatives when the majority of the flock could care less about a certain biblical interpretation, missions endeavor, or the latest gimmick for "church growth" from headquarters.

Overall, what was most troublesome to me was the church's neutrality and apathy in obeying and pursuing with all diligence three premiere commandments of the New Testament. *"Love the Lord your God with all your heart and with all your soul and with all your mind...Love your neighbor as yourself" (Matthew 22:37-39). "Therefore go and make disciples of all nations, baptizing them in the name of the Father and of the Son and of the Holy Spirit, and teaching them to obey everything I have commanded you. And surely I am with you always, to the very end of the age" (Matthew 28:19-20).* Simply put, Jesus implores us to love God and others. Further, the body of Christ is commanded to make disciples of all nations.

Certainly, these observations and impressions were brewing in me as I journeyed to a youth pastor's conference in March, 1992. Accompanying me to this conference were a couple of my youth pastor buddies including my comrade, Steve Smothers. Attending these types of conferences at the time served as a good diversion from my ministry schedule. I did not expect or anticipate God to show up in such a compelling way in my life. The conference speakers were transparent, challenging and "cutting edge." One of those speakers included an incredible servant, Dave Busby, who has since passed on. His pain has vanished as he worships continually with Jesus in heaven.

There was, however, a significant problem that I encountered at this conference. The worship team was a group of guys who I didn't care for. In previous years, I did not appreciate how they led for a youth camp that I directed. The problem was not theirs—it was mine. The problem was my attitude. I remember thinking, "If I can just coast through the times of worship and get to the speakers, then I'll be okay." God had different plans.

God's Spirit dealt with my poor attitude and past memories of this worship team. As a matter of fact, it was during a time of worship that God's presence landed on me. Isn't God creative? I desired to simply survive the worship and he decides to do something completely different with me in the course of worship. God gave to me a visual image or picture in my mind. Some may call this a vision. To me, indeed, I believe God did give me a vision. I saw a sea of humanity moving rapidly toward a great, bright light that resembled a throne upon which a king or leader would sit. The people approaching this throne were exuberant, full of life, and rushing enthusiastically to the throne. The environment was electric and filled with joy. A big smile splashed across my face. I wanted to run with these troopers to the throne.

In the blink of an eye, the scene dramatically shifted before me. The light that ascended from the throne was snuffed out. Darkness and gloom cast their ghastly shadows upon the once radiant runners to the throne. The people were stopped dead in their tracks and began a mournful and collective cry. They began to bellow at a darkened figure that was now transposed over the bleak throne. This darkened figure raised up his arms and the people's wailing ceased. Before me now was a horrific picture of hopelessness, oppression and despair. This freeze framed picture saddened my heart, my lips began to quiver, and I began to quietly cry. I thought, "Campbell, what is up with you, man? Are you losing it? I must be crazy!" Yet, I knew the author of the vision was God.

At this point, I recall being overwhelmed with His presence. I extended my arms toward my two youth pastor friends who were seated on my left and right and grabbed their arms. I quietly slumped to my seat because I felt I could no longer stand. I asked

Him, "What do I do now, God? Sit here like a buffoon?" I really did not have any plan of action as I was saturated in his profound presence. I sat and waited. This type of response is tough for a goal driven, "in-control" choleric like me.

After a few moments which seemed like hours had transpired, I sensed that I should open my Bible and read something. I turned to the Proverbs. I don't know why. The worship music continued in the background. Eventually, I made my way to *Proverbs 28:12* which reads, *"When the righteous triumph, there is great elation; but when the wicked rise to power, men go into hiding."* God was beginning the process of bringing some comprehension of his vision to me. I rapidly read through the rest of the chapter. I journeyed into the next chapter and centered in on Proverbs 29:1 which states, *"When the righteous thrive, the people rejoice; when the wicked rule, the people groan."* I was convinced that these two verses would help me come to grips with what He was communicating to me. These two verses are still marked in my tattered, preaching Bible.

I read these verses over and over again as the worship team continued to play. God, however, was not finished dealing with me. He spoke to the deepest part of my heart and spirit saying, "You will plant a church." This directive from God was the farthest thing from my mind. I was happy with the ministry that God had entrusted me to lead and oversee. I had never discussed planting a church with my wife. The conference's theme was not about church planting. "Where did this come from? Is this God speaking to me or just my own personal hallucination?" were the questions rolling through my mind. I remember chuckling, shrugging my shoulders in disbelief, and kneeling down on the floor in the limited space between the chairs.

I prayed a simple prayer. "God, if this is you, then confirm these words to me by filling me with your peace." My anxiety and unsettled spirit lifted immediately. I continued to pray. "God, if this is you, then confirm these words through those who are close to me." I felt very assured that my wife and close ministry associates would clear things up for me and I would continue my youth pastorate as if nothing ever happened. The worship came to an abrupt end, I sat in my chair, and the speaker began.

Before I continue, let me investigate some potential feelings that you might be having as you have read this vision experience.

First, I am not a mystic. I had never before received a vision from God. Further, my "theological construct" did not lean toward this type of experience with God. I had heard numerous people speak about visions from God. I continually was skeptical about these ooey-gooey assertions about "God speaking to individuals through visions or dreams." People who are close to me will tell you that I am not the kind of individual who acts, communicates or lives in a mystical realm. I am a very simple man.

I came to grips with my simplicity recently during a ministry trip to Zimbabwe. Patrick Mpande, the overseer of Victory Life Ministries, introduced me to his people who were crowded into a circus tent for their annual "Camp Meeting." He stated, "This man, Rob Campbell, who is about to speak to you comes from America. He is a Texan. Everything is big in Texas. Rob leads a big church. During my trips to Wimberley, Texas, I have watched Cypress Creek Church grow like you wouldn't believe. This church is awesome. I couldn't understand why this church was so powerful in the kingdom of God. So, I asked God. God told me that one reason Cypress Creek Church was powerful is that the primary leader was not fancy or complicated. God was teaching me about Rob Campbell. This man, Pastor Rob, is a simple man. God taught me that through simplicity, there is great power."

I have been introduced before a speaking engagement on numerous occasions. Patrick's introduction of me before my dear friends in Zimbabwe seemed odd. As I stepped to the microphone, I thought, "You know, Rob, you are not a genius. You're not brilliant. You have nothing to offer these people today in your own power. Indeed, you are just a simple man." I cherish these words from Patrick and embrace them today.

Second, I'm not overly impressed with individuals who approach me with a typical line like, "Brother, I got a word from God for you." Frequently, their faces exude a far-off, distant look. They speak "Christian-ese" and don't lift my spirit. They are spooky to me. Frankly, I sense that many of these troopers are self-proclaimed "messengers from God" that parade around enticed by the grand charade that they are important—really important—to God. Don't get me wrong. I do believe in, have received, and have dispensed prophecies from God. I long for God, however, to be the center of such miraculous transactions and not the messenger.

Moreover, as a conservative, analytical thinker, this vision from God challenged my perception of God. He was changing my thoughts about his supernatural modes of operation with me. Indeed, God had given me a vision and spoke to me specifically and clearly about beginning a church. *Joel 2:28* became a great comfort to me. *"I will pour out my Spirit on all people. Your sons and daughters will prophesy, your old men will dream dreams, your young men will see visions."*

As the conference speaker continued his talk, I began wrestling with God. I asked God, "Who is the darkened figure that ascended the throne and cast oppression upon the people. Is this person a man, a pastor...my pastor? Was I the oppressive one? Is this figure the enemy?" God continued to speak revealing to me that the dreary figure was not a sole individual or Satan, but the general and collective leaders of the body of Christ. This revelation made perfect sense to me for I longed for God's people (ordinary people) to be released to minister in their giftedness, pursuing fruitfulness and fulfillment in the kingdom of God. This revelation also brought comfort to me. I really did not want God to say, "This figure is Pastor 'so and so.' This figure is your church. This figure symbolizes the future of your ministry." Most assuredly, God was calling me to be a change agent concerning the current state of affairs in the body of Christ. He was calling me to begin a new church. He was leading me to be the type of leader who would empower people to pursue his presence and experience his power. He wanted to use me so that a portion of his body might experience *"great elation"* and *"rejoice"* in him. A deep sense of humility covered me. I began to dialogue with God about my inadequacies, lack of knowledge concerning the word and spiritual matters, and my own personal satisfaction with my ministry with youth. Needless to say, I didn't catch a word that flowed from the mouth of the conference speaker, but I did hear God speak.

As I departed the conference meeting room, I turned to Steve and said to him, "When we get back to the hotel, I REALLY need to talk with you." I was safe. Certainly, Steve would not confirm or encourage me in this vision. I could simply rest in the fact that God did something in my life that was neat, but could be set aside until a later date. I could carry on with the youth ministry that God had called me to and life would go on.

I was wrong. Steve listened intently with great fervor concerning my experience with God. As I discussed the preposterous thought of planting a church, Steve gently spoke into my life. "Rob," he stated, "God is going to use you for big things. His call and plan for your life is bigger, much bigger than what you can accomplish in your own strength, creativity and ingenuity. He has revealed to you his desire for you and you must pursue this with wisdom and spiritual accountability." I received these words from Steve, but I knew that God would not be able to convince my wife that church planting would be in our imminent future.

The conference ended and we headed home. As we traveled, I remembered a commitment that my wife and I had made before God. When we moved in 1988 to Wimberley, Texas, we both sensed that God had called us to this place of ministry for life. How could I plant a new church in the same small Texas town where I had been engaged in youth ministry for the last five years? In no way did I sense that God was going to parachute me into another community and begin a new church. I had no peace about this scenario. Life was good in Wimberley. We loved our church, the community, and enjoyed the security of my present ministry position. I rested in the fact that God would have to orchestrate this plan in my family's life. He would first have to work on my best friend and life partner, my wife, Susan.

I was safe. As I pulled into the driveway of my home, I prayed, "God, I want this charge from you to be about you. I don't want to do this church planting thing. I know that Susan will be strongly opposed to this notion. You're going to have to speak to Susan." In retrospect, this prayer was a challenge from me to God for Him to continue to work in my life. I walked into our home, embraced my wife and our three-year old daughter, Taylor. We spent some time reconnecting with each other. We ate dinner, cleaned up the dishes, and bathed the kid. We placed Taylor in her bed. I sat down in my recliner, picked up the newspaper, and began to emotionally unwind.

Susan walked into the living room and asked me, "So, are you going to tell me or am I going to have to wait until tomorrow?" I really didn't want to meticulously recant all that I had experienced with God the past few days at this time. I responded, "I'll tell you what. Let's just talk about it tomorrow. I'm tired and you're tired. You don't want to hear it all now, do you?" I just knew that Susan would agree to wait until the next day. It didn't happen. "No," she replied, "If you're ready to talk, I'd love to hear about what God spoke to you right now."

God opened the door and I had no option but to walk through this door and begin to explain my experience to her. The hours passed like minutes. During the course of this dialogue, I began to realize that not only was Susan intrigued with my experience, she was genuinely excited about God speaking to me. This reality shocked me. I was the risk taker, the adventurer. Susan was the careful, methodical and cautious partner provided by God to keep me grounded. As I watched God's enthusiasm in Susan begin to blossom, His enthusiasm in me begin to burst forth. The conversation with my wife was incredible, dynamic and fun. Susan asked insightful and penetrating questions. We wrestled honestly before God and with each other. The conversation came to a close when Susan stated, "Well, let's talk again tomorrow. I need some time to ponder this whole deal." I responded, "You bet. Susan, I want you to know one last thing. I will not go down this road without your full support and blessing. We are a team. Take your time, ask as many questions as you need, and we'll just see what happens."

As the days progressed, Susan and I sensed that God was calling us to plant a new church in Wimberley. God's vision for us began to burn deeper in our hearts. Genuine excitement about joining God, taking this risk, and planting a healthy, dynamic church began to consume our thoughts. As we journeyed together in this process, I remembered the word of counsel I had received from Steve. He said to me, "You must pursue this with wisdom and spiritual accountability." The Lord gave to Steve incredible insight in those words of counsel to me. I must continually allow God's wisdom to lead me and remain accountable to those who afforded me spiritual protection. The next step was to share what God was up to in my life with my fellow pastors in the church where I served as youth pastor.

Many hours of dialogue ensued with my dear friends on the pastoral staff at the church. I desperately needed and desired their counsel. They walked with me as the circle of counsel expanded to key leaders in the church and region. The obvious peculiarities of this call upon my life were openly dissected, probed and discussed. Overall, this cluster of friends and ministry associates confirmed God's leading in my life. We labored in the atmosphere of inter-dependence to extend the kingdom of God and enhance the spiritual climate in this region of the world. I am grateful to these men and women to this day. *"Plans fail for lack of counsel, but with many advisers they succeed" (Proverbs 15:22).* These advisers encouraged, blessed and released me to pursue the planting of a new church in Wimberley, Texas. The "Gamaliel" approach to this new initiative was overtly presented. *"For if their purpose or activity is of human origin, it will fail. But if it is from God, you will not be able to stop these men; you will only find yourselves fighting against God" (Acts 5:38-b-39).*

I do not want to present a picture that every aspect of this new church plant fell precisely in place. This was not the case. Every notable character in the scriptures faced opposition as he/she pursued God's vision and directive. Just as Nehemiah had his Sanballat and Tobiah, I had my fair share of opposition and perse-cution. One man told a friend of mine that I "had fallen off the deep end." In my transition from youth ministry to church planting, however, I never experienced one not-yet believer chastising me for planting a new church in town. Frankly, the majority of not-yet believers that I consistently communicated with were sincerely interested in, and supportive of, this new endeavor in my life. The majority of these individuals have since received Christ and many are now leaders in the church today. Cutting to the chase, my main opposition and persecution came from churched folks. I repeatedly wanted to defend myself and the process. I never did and here is why. In December of 1992, God spoke to me through the following scripture: *"He who loves a pure heart and whose speech is gracious will have the king for his friend" (Proverbs 22:11).* I knew that God was my defense, refuge and strong tower. My responsibility before God was to be gracious in my words and pure in my heart. These were my specific marching orders from God. I could not and would not sway from these principles.

Moreover, many of the personal attacks that were levied against me by church folks in the planting of a new church were cast my way by misinformed individuals. The large majority of these Sanballats and Tobiahs were not even residing in Wimberley, Texas. They did not know me. These attacks, however, were a means for God to work in a deeper way in MY life. I believe that everything that comes into my life is Father-filtered. He allows persecution, personal attacks and offenses to occur for one primary reason—the continual refinement of my character. His refining fire was operative in my life to test my resolve and commitment to his vision and call in my life. Would I self-destruct amidst the attacks or increase my dependence upon him? Would I puff up and retaliate or would I rest in the shadow of his strong tower? He taught me that church planting is a spiritual act. He must increase and I must decrease. He did not need me, but chose to use me.

Concurrent with the opposition mentioned above, there were familial challenges. Beginning January 1, 1993, I would have no income. I did not sense that God was leading me to search out potential funds from mission agencies, various denominations, or churches in the region. I believe strongly that church planters greatly benefit in life if they look to the marketplace for money to pay their bills and feed their family. I immediately pursued a job at a local outlet mall. I was a cashier. I remember my wife and mother-in-law coming to a tent sale that the store where I worked was hosting. There I stood ringing up the purchases of the customers behind the cash register. I was pulling down $5.00 an hour and having a blast. I loved mixing it up with ordinary folks and not-yet believers. I will never forget the look on my mother-in-law's face as I rang up her purchases. Her non-verbals were shouting, "What in the world is my son-in-law doing? Has he lost his mind? A college graduate with a pre-law degree working as a cash register operator!" As my wife approached the check out counter, a smile splashed across her face. I'm sure she was enjoying the fact that I had a "real" job, but the smile meant more to me. The smile was laced with an assurance that everything was going to be alright.

In my initial pursuit to survive financially, I secured a job selling Cutco knives. I was trained on how to sell the products with intense concentration given to closing the deal. I discovered I was a lousy salesman. I sold a few knives—mainly to relatives! I secured odd jobs around town in my effort to make a buck. I was also in the process of finishing a Masters in Education with a concentration in family and marriage counseling. I sought out a licensed professional counselor who was a Christian and began a small counseling practice under her covering. The practice grew at a brisk pace as I counseled fifteen clients a week during the evening hours. Eventually, as Cypress Creek Church began to grow, the faithful core committed some financial support to me. I was extremely grateful to these men and women who were excited about God's activity in our midst. I was working three jobs and my income was 60% less than what I had received the previous year. Then, God intervened.

His intervention, however, was not what you might expect. Let me explain. A local business center had some space freed up which used to house our town's feed store. I called the landlord and asked about the possibility of leasing this space that would accommodate the church for Celebration services on Sunday mornings and provide administrative offices. He conveyed to me what it would cost to secure the space. The amount of money needed for the security deposit and the first month's rent matched precisely what Susan and I had in our savings account. The old saying rushed through my mind. "Do you trust God or just say that you trust God?" We determined that the space was God's plan for CCC, emptied out our savings account, and secured the space. This intervention from God was a further test of my family's faith in Him.

In the first two months of CCC life, he had grown the body (the first cell of CCC) from an initial core of forty-three people to approximately one-hundred fifty individuals. We gathered only on Sunday nights in a home. I felt like I was a part of a Chinese house church with the living room, den, kitchen, and bedrooms packed with people. Literally, people (mainly children and youth) were peering through the windows of the home to hear the teachings and participate in our crude and uncomplicated attempt to worship with an out of tune guitar. For many in this initial cell, this was their first taste of Christian community. Heart-to-heart connections were being fused by God's Spirit among the family units present. People were receiving Christ, relationships were being restored with God, physical healings occurred, and LIFE permeated the church. In March 1993, this initial cell multiplied and gave birth to triplets. Further, we began Celebration on Sunday mornings at Wimberley Mountain Plaza after some hard labor (and a lot of laughs) in transforming the feed store into a worship center.

This first year of CCC was the most exhilarating and challenging year of my life. Susan and I laughed in disbelief every two weeks when I would write the checks to pay the bills. During this year, God allowed us to refinance our house, add a sunroom to our home, and purchase a new (used) vehicle for Susan. I can't make the financial figures work to this day. Truly, we experienced God's miraculous plan of economy. Additionally, our home became a refuge and support base for a family member who needed a place to finish his high school career. We grew together as a married couple and family. Every turn in the road was fresh, exciting and intriguing.

During these initial months of CCC life, God spoke to Susan. God speaks in a variety of ways including his Word, his Spirit, circumstances, and through other people. On this occasion, Susan was listening to a popular song sung by a Christian artist. A portion of the song speaks of "peace without understanding." Susan thought, "That's it. This is my experience right now. I don't fully understand what God is doing, but I am filled with peace." Indeed, God's peace consumed us.

As the years have unfolded, Jesus remains the head of the church. We have watched God bring hundreds to salvation. We have seen him heal marriages and restore dysfunctional families. We have seen him raise up ordinary people (simple folks!) to lead in extraordinary ways. Over one hundred adults, youth and children now Shepherd the cells of the body. We have joined God's heartbeat in planting churches in this region and overseas. Can you imagine my joy when Steve Smothers said, "Yes!" to my invitation for him to pastor our first church plant, Dripping Springs Community Fellowship? God has provided hundreds of thousands of dollars to ministries, missionaries and pastors in foreign countries. Through the faithful troopers of CCC, God allowed us to build a physical home for the spiritual family. God has lifted people from within CCC to serve as pastors and overseers. We have participated with him in his desire to establish an environment of grace.

Additionally, I have experienced the words of Jesus stated in *John 15:5, "I am the vine; you are the branches. If a man remains in me, and I in him, he will bear much fruit; apart from me you can do nothing."* I know to the core of my being that it is *"not by might nor by power, but by my spirit" (Zechariah 4:6)* that God builds the church. Consequently, I am humbled by his presence and power in our midst.

As my confession to you, please know that I have made many mistakes. I have hurt people as I have led. I have thought that my plan, ideas and initiatives were better than the Father's desires for me and this church. The longer I live and lead, the more I realize that the culmination of all I know pales to God's wisdom. I am not a perfect person or a perfect leader. God has not called me to be perfect but complete in Him. This completion is worked out moment by moment, day by day.

I have just shared with you a historical parcel of my journey with God. In the pages that follow, you will discover countless stories of those individuals that make up CCC. Additionally, I will be sharing numerous stories from various pockets of the globe depicting the moving of God's hand upon the church today. You will see God's activity in our midst. You will discover how God is telling, shaping and forming His-story through ordinary vessels throughout the world. *"For the eyes of the Lord range throughout the earth to strengthen those whose hearts are fully committed to him" (2 Chronicles 16:9a).*

Chapter Three

"A Matter of Life and Death"

George Turklebaum worked at the same desk in the same firm for thirty years. He shared the open-plan work environment with twenty three other workers. In mid December, 2000, George quietly passed away at the early age of 51. Elliot Wachiaski, George's boss, stated, "George was always the first guy in each morning and the last to leave at night. He was always absorbed in his work and kept much to himself."

Just an ordinary passing you might think. No, not really. You see, George passed away on a Monday at his office desk, but nobody noticed until Saturday morning when an office cleaner asked why he was still working during the weekend. A post-mortem examination revealed that George had been dead for five days after suffering a coronary. Ironically, George was proofreading manuscripts of medical textbooks when he died.[15]

This bizarre and morbid scenario conjures up many emotions within me. I feel desperately sad, bitterly confused and admittedly angry. Why didn't anyone notice that George remained lifeless at this desk for several days? Day after day his fellow employees passed by his desk in their usual hurry to accomplish their assigned tasks and greeted him with a flippant, "Good morning, George." Yet this generic, heartless, traditional greeting fell on deaf—or dead—ears.

It would be safe to assume that George's fellow office mates had little connection with him. He may have been a common fixture like Norm or Cliff at "Cheers." He was always around and no one really knew him, just his name. You might further assume that George was not the life of the office. He was not the office clown exchanging stock tips or the latest joke at the water cooler. He showed up to work, plopped himself down at this desk, did his work, went home and repeated the mundane cycle for approximately nine thousand days of his life.

This real to life scenario illustrates the state of the American church. We are dead and few within our environment are taking notice. Behind our desks, we are working repetitious and monotonous tasks, pouring over manuals of how to do church, having little connection with our fellow journeymen in this life. We are, however, consistent. We show up. We sing. We listen. We spectate. And then we repeat the cycle week after week with little life change. We are self-absorbed in a self-absorbed culture. We are dead at our desk waiting for the clean up crew to take notice.

Some American churches are searching for life, trying to change—for change's sake. They are desperately searching for ways to appear alive, "with it," hip, "in touch," connected. They are enticed by gimmicks laced with foolishness in an effort to look vivacious. Consider this experience by a Florida man and his wife.

A man was working on his motorcycle on his patio and his wife was in the kitchen. The man was racing the engine on the motorcycle when it accidentally slipped into gear. The man, still holding on to the handle bars, was dragged through the glass patio doors and along with the motorcycle dumped onto the floor inside the house.

The wife, hearing the crash, ran into the dining room and found her husband laying on the floor, cut and bleeding, the motorcycle laying next to him and the shattered patio door. The wife ran to the phone and summoned an ambulance. After the ambulance arrived and transported the man to the hospital, the wife up righted the motorcycle and pushed it outside. Since gas was spilled on the floor, the wife got some paper towels, blotted up the gasoline, and threw the towels in the toilet. The husband was treated and released to come home.

Upon arriving home, he looked at the shattered patio door and the damage done to his motorcycle. He became despondent, went to the bathroom, sat down on the toilet and smoked a cigarette. After finishing the cigarette, he flipped it between his legs into the toilet bowl while still seated.

The wife, who was in the kitchen, heard the loud explosion and her husband screaming. She ran into the bathroom and found her husband lying on the floor. His trousers had been blown away and he was suffering burns on the buttocks, the back of his legs and his groin. The wife again ran to the phone to call the ambulance. The very same paramedic crew was dispatched and the wife met them at the street. The paramedics loaded the husband on the stretcher and began carrying him to the street. While they were going down the stairs to the street, accompanied by the wife, one of the paramedics asked the wife how the husband had burned himself. She told them and the paramedics started laughing so hard, one of them slipped and tipped the stretcher, dumping the husband out. He fell down the remaining stairs and broke his arm.

As the church revs her motor, silliness, needless destruction, dead works, life shattering episodes, fires and explosions are left in the vestige. The emergency crew of church growth experts arrive on the scene doing their best to grant care and comfort, but quietly shake their heads in disbelief and bewilderment, fending off a devilish belly full of laughter.

Many churches have turned to people instead of God in their pursuit to obtain new life for their fledgling flock. God is saying, "Turn to me. I am LIFE." The church, however, turns a deaf ear and eventually surrenders to a well known church consultant who desires to come in and make sense of things. I recently heard the following story which parallels this notion.

A shepherd was herding his flocks in a remote pasture when suddenly a brand new Jeep Cherokee advanced out of a dust cloud towards him. The driver, a young man in a Versaci suit, Gucci shoes, Ray Ban sunglasses and a YSL tie leaned out of the window and asked the shepherd, "If I can tell you exactly how many sheep you have in your flock, will you give me one?" The shepherd looks at the yuppie, then at his peacefully grazing flock and calmly answers "Sure!"

The yuppie parks the car, whips out his notebook, connects it to a cell-phone, surfs to a NASA page on the Internet where he calls up a GPS satellite navigation system, scans the area, opens up a database and some 60 Excel spreadsheets with complex formulas. Finally, he prints out a 150 page report on his hi-tech miniaturized printer, turns around to our shepherd and says "You have here exactly 1586 sheep!" "This is correct. As agreed, you can take one of the sheep," says the shepherd. He watches the young man make a selection and bundle it in his Cherokee. Then he says, "If I can tell you exactly what your business is, will you give me my sheep back?" "Okay, why not," answers the young man. "You are a consultant," says the shepherd. "This is correct," says the yuppie, "How did you guess that?" "Easy," answers the shepherd, "You turn up here although nobody called you. You want to be paid for the answer to a question I already knew the solution to. And you don't know anything about my business because you took my dog."

People may be curious about God, but they have closed the curtains on the church. Robert Nash, Jr., writes, "The number one religious story of the next century will be the deaths of thousands of local Christian churches."[16] Is this statement to you prophetic or pathetic? Is it anointed or annoying? Does it cause you to be angry? Does it offend you? Do you find yourself happy that some-one who loves the church like Nash had the guts to proclaim such an assertion?

Personally, I don't like this brash, bold and blatant prognostica-tion, but I believe it. The handwriting is on the wall. The statistics indicate severe decline. The church needs respiration. Nash is not alone in his assessment of the current state of affairs. "We must accept that the traditional place of the institutional church in American society is dying," argues Mike Regele in his book *Death of the Church*, "and with it the institutional church itself."[17] Kenneth L. Woodward writes on the subject *"Dead End for the Mainline?"* that "From every angle Protestantism is gripped by crisis: of identity and loyalty, membership and money, leadership and organization, cultures and belief."[18] Pastor Cesar Castellanos

(International Charismatic Mission, Bogota, Colombia) suggests that the North American church is like a man who bought his wife a beautiful home and all the best things to fill it. Then she became entertained with all the things and put her husband out of the house. "That is the condition of the American church," he heard the Lord say, "They have kept MY things, but they have pushed ME out, and I am on the outside."

Thomas Boomershine offers this analogy of the church reflecting upon Hitler's blitzkrieg and the Polish army in September, 1939:

> Hitler sent 14 armored divisions across the Polish border. The Polish army was committed to the traditions of the cavalry and sent 12 cavalry brigades against the German tanks. In the tradition of the great cavalry divisions of the Prussian army, the Polish cavalry was molded for warfare as it had been fought in the 18th and 19th century. When the divisions of German armor came streaming across the border, therefore, the Polish generals sent wave after wave of cavalry, men mounted on horses, against the tanks. The battle lasted about three weeks. The fields of Poland were choked with the bodies of horses and brave men who had gone into battle with a strategy formed for warfare in a previous period.
>
> Today the church goes into spiritual battle in an electronic culture, seeking to communicate the gospel in a new cultural environment. In a culture dominated by television, films, CDs, and computers, the Church continues to pursue its strategies that were developed for a culture in which books, journals, and rhetorical addresses were the most powerful means of mass communication.
>
> Like the Polish cavalry, [mainline Protestant churches] are dying in this culture...empty and abandoned Protestant churches [strewn across] America's landscape like the horses and men of the Polish cavalry on the fields of Poland.[19]

Richard Halverson writes: "When faith began in Palestine, it began with a relationship with a person, it moved to Greece and became a philosophy, it moved to Rome and became an institution, it moved to Europe and became a culture, it moved to the U.S. and became an enterprise." The U.S. church enterprise seems to be falling short. Tommy Tenney writes, *"The bottom line is that people are sick of church because the Church has been somewhat less than what the Book advertised. People want to connect with a higher power."*[20] Church attendance in the U.S. is at an all time low. One-third of U.S. churches never grow beyond 50 members; two-thirds never grow beyond 150 members; and only 5 percent grow beyond 350 members.[21]

In relation to the state of the church, some see the glass half full. Some see the glass as empty. Others simply see another glass that needs to be washed. Let me make myself clear. I am hopeful, enthusiastic and filled with anticipation that God is and will bring new life into the American church. In essence, this book highlights this belief at the core of my heart. Yes, I am an optimist—an eternal optimist for the "gates of hell shall not prevail." Recently, through a series of encounters, God drilled home this hopeful anticipation to me. Let me explain.

Because I pastor a very young congregation, I do many more baby dedications than hospital visits or funerals. I am thankful. On a recent night, however, I journeyed to the hospital with a fellow pastor, Jim Donaldson, and found Brian and his lovely wife, Tina. Brian's father was critically ill. He had fallen the day before and was suffering from internal bleeding in his brain area. As we approached the hospital room, Brian greeted us with a friendly hug, explained that his Dad was in his final hours, and escorted us briskly into the room where his father laid. Brian said, "C'mon in here and pray with my Dad." I will not soon forget Brian's actions and words that ensued. He leaned over the bed and pressed his mouth near his father's ear and said, "Dad, Pastor Rob and Pastor Jim are here to pray with you. You remember our pastors, don't you Dad? You have met them and they are here to pray with you. Dad, very soon you will be with Jesus. You are passing on to be with Jesus forever, Dad. Soon you will not be in pain. You will be with Jesus, Dad. Your family and friends are here, Dad. Pastor Rob is going to pray with us all, Dad."

Hands were joined around the bed and I felt very inadequate. I prayed. I cannot specifically recall what I prayed, but I know that I prayed for comfort, peace and understanding. Tears were shed, and I sympathized with the family and friends that were gathered in the sterile, cold hospital room as I perused the pain stricken faces. Meshed with the pain of the obvious state of affairs, there was something greater that I sensed. Surprisingly, I discovered hope and joy.

Hope collided with pain and birthed joy. *"Hope deferred makes the heart sick, but a longing fulfilled is a tree of life" (Proverbs 13:12).* Joy was present that Brian's dad was passing on in the presence of his family and close friends. *"Do not grieve, for the joy of the Lord is your strength" (Nehemiah 8:10b).* Those attending to this passing on rested in the hope that this beloved father, grandfather and friend would be with Christ for eternity. A few hours later, the life support was removed from Brian's dad. He didn't pass on immediately, but eventually his physical shell expired and he was ushered into heaven. I came to the hospital to minister and I left being ministered to. But this is just half the story.

A few days passed and hundreds of people gathered for the funeral. The church was packed. As we say in the South, the church was "as full as a tick." The place was hot. As a matter of fact, I remember standing during the funeral and singing a traditional hymn and feeling lightheaded. I shed my jacket, made it through the singing and quickly took my seat. Following the service, people mixed and mingled in the rear of the sanctuary that doubled as a fellowship hall. Hugs, tears, and memories were shared.

The very next Sunday, Brian and his family decided to worship in his parent's church—the same church that had just received hundreds of people for the funeral. On this Sunday morning, however, the atmosphere was drastically different. Besides Brian and his family, only twelve other people were present for worship.

Brian recalled this experience to me over breakfast at the town café the very next week. I could not believe it! I stopped him abruptly and said, "Wait a minute, Brian. Did I hear you say that only twelve other people were present for worship?" He confirmed what I thought I heard him say. Sadness filled my heart. The greatest tool of the enemy (discouragement) began to creep into my spirit. I had to change the subject quickly. And I did. But, this memory lingers in my mind until this very day.

"What a picture of the current state of affairs," I thought. Hundreds come out to honor a beloved man, but the sanctuary is all but abandoned the very next Sunday. The building and grounds look well kept, but the spirit of the church is empty and hollow. The funeral attendees shared in the family's pain and extended words of consolation, yet death flutters over this part of the body of Christ. In the midst of remembering and honoring the dead on the day of the funeral, life buzzed through the fortress. On the following Sunday, however, life is nowhere to be found. Hope and joy fill a hospital room and church is a pain on Sunday morning.

I believe that the majority of American churches are hollow and empty. A story by a masterful storyteller and former U.S. President, Abraham Lincoln, provides an intriguing metaphor for this assertion. Let me explain. At one point during the war, Lincoln was forced by his cabinet to confront the realization that many people who were thought to be Union patriots were actually spies providing key information to the Confederacy. As was his custom, Lincoln calmed the fears of his zealous and accusative cabinet members by telling the following story of an old farmer who had a very large shade tree towering over his house.

It was a majestic-looking tree, and apparently perfect in every part—tall, straight, and of immense size—the grand old sentinel of his forest home. One morning, while at work in his garden, he saw a squirrel [run up the tree into a hole] and thought the tree might be hollow. He proceeded to examine it carefully and, much to his surprise, he found that the stately [tree] that he had [valued] for its beauty and grandeur to be the pride and protection of his little farm was hollow from top to bottom. Only a rim of sound wood remained, barely sufficient to support its weight. What was he to do? If he cut it down, it would [do great damage] with its great length and spreading branches. If he let it remain, his family was in constant danger. In a storm it might fall, or the wind might blow it down, and his house and children be crushed by it. What should he do? As he turned away, he said sadly, "I wish I had never seen that squirrel."[22]

Which American churches will face the hollow nature of their existence? Will we turn our heads disregarding the squirrels? The majestic-looking tree that provided the pleasant shade for the farmer and his family becomes a metaphor for the appearance of life and death in the church today.

Dorman Duggan knows about this type of metaphor in the church. In 1973, after being expelled from a fundamentalist church because of theological differences, Dorman and his family began a church in his home. Many Christians from area churches flocked to this new church plant. A plurality of leadership was developed and a Christian school began. Contemporary means of worshiping God were implemented. This new church, however, was not developing well. The church was plagued with pain, unforgiveness and hurt. The church's structure was hindering growth and development. Dorman knew that "things were going down hill," and a fresh change was on the horizon.

Sensing that God desired a fresh start after seventeen tumultuous years, Dorman believed that the old had to die. *"Unless a kernel of wheat falls to the ground and dies, it remains only a single seed. But if it dies, it produces many seeds" (John 12:24)*. God was asking Dorman to lead the church in dealing with unforgiveness in the people's lives. God's heart ached over the area churches that experienced hurt when Dorman and his crew began the church with great zeal "not caring who [they] hurt or received from other churches." God was calling this church to repentance.

How would Dorman respond to God's movement in his life concerning the faulty and contentious foundation of this church plant? Dorman remembered that crucifixion (or death) preceded resurrection. Dorman believed that God was asking him to hold a funeral service for the church. Yes, a funeral service! With great courage, Dorman shared this idea with his leadership team who agreed with this initiative. Plans were made to bury the church.

As the people of the church gathered for the worship service, a small coffin positioned in the worship center was quite noticeable. A small wicker basket (shaped like a coffin) was placed on the communion table. Dorman began the funeral service speaking of God's judgments against the leadership of the church, offenses between the members, and somberly read God's reconciliation plan from *Matthew 18*. Collectively, the church asked God's forgiveness for the disunity that was present among the churches of the region. Dorman asked each person present to write down on a slip of paper all the debts that they felt someone owed them. The slips of paper were placed in the coffin shaped basket as a symbolic act to "burn and bury all unforgiveness." As the people paraded one by one to the communion table to release these debts, Dorman sensed that God's spirit was moving among the people as many sought forgiveness from fellow church members. Once again as a symbolic act of death, the slips of paper were bundled together, burned and buried behind the church building. This church, birthed in 1973, was now proclaimed dead.

Dorman now pastors a new church in the same town with the very same people from this previous church. Not one member or leader left the church following this funeral service. Dorman suggests, "I think there are a lot of churches that need to do this, but I believe tradition and pride are hard things to kill." What a courageous act! A pastor leading his people to experience the painfully obvious—a church who desperately needed resurrection LIFE. God desires that his people be full of life. *"I have come that you may have LIFE, and have it to the full...I am the resurrection and the LIFE...I am the way and the truth and the LIFE...Choose LIFE!"* *(John 10:10,11:25,14:6; Duet. 30:19)*.

Years ago, one of my fellow Overseers at Cypress Creek Church, John Ellis, reminded me that "life is irony." Look at the irony of *2 Corinthians 4:10-12* which reads, *"We always carry around in our body the death of Jesus, so that the life of Jesus may also be revealed in our body. For we who are alive are always being given over to death for Jesus' sake, so that his life may be revealed in our mortal body. So then, death is at work in us, but life is at work in you."*

Death, my friends, precedes life. In the natural realm, this may be a surprising statement to many. The Apostle Paul, however, helps us to understand this spiritual interplay between life and death. *"The body that is sown is perishable, it is raised imperishable; it is sown in dishonor, it is raised in glory; it is sown in weakness, it is raised in power, it is sown a natural body, it is raised a spiritual body" (I Corinthians 15:42-44a).*

Jesus stated, *"If anyone would come after me, he must deny himself and take up his cross daily and follow me. For whoever wants to save his life will lose it, but whoever loses his life for me will find it" (Luke 9:23, Matthew 16:25).* The cross is the only way that God ever does anything of value in your life. Anything that comes into your life that bypasses the cross will be temporal, not eternal. The challenge, therefore, for thousands of churches who are desperately yearning for life is to return to the cross. Specifically, we must repent from DEAD works so that we might experience life.

Hebrews 6:1-3 is the clarion call to the church today. In this passage, God presents to us six foundational truths which the author deems to be "elementary" in our journey with God. The first two foundations are repentance from dead works and faith toward God. Remember, you enter into the kingdom of God through repentance and faith. Further, you grow as a believer through repentance and faith. Let's ponder for a few moments this call to repentance.

My desire for you is to see repentance as a gift from God. *"Every good and perfect GIFT is from above, coming down from the Father of the heavenly lights, who does not change like shifting shadows" (James 1:17).* Every time you choose to repent you become more like Jesus. Repentance is a change of mind and attitude leading to a change of behavior. Repentance is rooted in a heart that aspires to please God. A repentant heart is a sign that one is dead to self and alive in Christ. True repentance is coupled with thrusting one's faith toward God.

I believe repentance is misunderstood and under-valued in the church today. Many Christians believe they have participated in repentance if they run to the altar during the invitation, weep about their careless ways, and emote their deepest secrets to God.

Repentance is not conviction of sin or the feeling of guilt or shame. Repentance is not outwardly reforming our lives in a deceptive crusade to look "together." Repentance is not being religious for one can be religious without changing his/her ways. Repentance is not penance whereby we try to pay for our own sins through good works. Further, repentance is not feeling sorry when we get caught for doing wrong.

As an example, my four-year old daughter has me wrapped around her little finger. I confess this to you. In recent months, she has picked up the phrase, "I'm sorry, daddy [or mommy or sissy referring to her older sibling]." Kayley is full of energy and in her never ending pursuit of play, there are times when plants, decorations and such get knocked over. She understands that the destruction of such property is not a good thing. On one occasion, as she somersaulted her way through the living room, a plant was toppled over by her lanky legs. She jumped to her feet quickly and peered into my face quietly waiting for my response. I simply looked at her rich, blue eyes. As our eyes locked on each other, she coyly stated, "I'm s-thory daddy!" She then quickly spun around and continued her aerobic workout.

Now, I'll be the first to confess that I don't know everything about parenting. I do believe, however, that it is safe to assume that her heart was not experiencing deep sorrow concerning her carelessness in toppling the house plant. As I teamed up with Kayley to upright the plant and retrieve the vacuum cleaner to clean up the dirt, God whispered to me. "Rob, this is how you come to me with your mess-ups." I momentarily act sorry and then carry on somersaulting my way through life. True repentance is lacking and I flippantly am repeating what I have heard others say, "I'm sorry God." *"Godly sorrow brings repentance that leads to salvation and leaves no regret, but worldly sorrow brings death" (2 Corinthians 7:10).* True repentance is life giving; worldly sorrow rooted in feelings of deep regret, hopelessness and despair brings death.

The cross reminds us that we cannot save ourselves. We must repent from our dead works. Now, let's think for a moment about this phrase "dead works." Before coming to Christ, who were you depending upon? Some would say, "Me! I depended on myself."

Some folks were dependent upon others. Notice who is absent from the equation—Jesus Christ! Everything we did in our lives before coming to Christ is considered dead works. *Galatians 2:20* states, *"I have been crucified with Christ and I no longer live, but Christ lives in me. The life I live in the body, I live by faith in the Son of God, who loved me and gave himself for me."*

Pointedly, dead works are anything that one does which is not initiated or energized by God. The motivational roots for dead works include misdirected zeal, guilty conscience, and self-promotion. Most assuredly, the American church is infused with dead works.

A pastor friend of mine had the occasion to spend some time in an informal setting with a small group of youth pastors from various churches. He was called in by this group to provide some counsel and serve as a mentor to these zealous troopers. He began to dialogue about the necessity to follow God in every youth ministry initiative. Eventually, he taught these young bucks about dead works. He posed the following question, "What percent of the ministry initiatives or programs that you led in the last year would fall into the category of dead works?" After a minute of silent reflection, one youth pastor responded by saying, "80%." The next youth pastor confidently stated, "At least 70% of my ministry initiatives were clearly in the dead works category." Finally, a third youth pastor hesitantly stated with heavy remorse in his voice, "95%." Dead works have permeated the church and prevail as the modus operandi in doing church.

The origin of dead works and life can be found in *Genesis 2* and *3*. Two trees were present in the Garden of Eden, the tree of the knowledge of good and evil, and the tree of life. The fruit of the first tree is death couched in the context of who is right and who is wrong. The fruit of the next tree is life couched in the context of life and death. As mentioned previously, God desires life for you and me. He desires LIFE for his people. His only Son died for us to know and experience LIFE. Unfortunately, the majority of American churches are eating (and living) the fruit off the wrong tree. Let me illustrate the profound difference between these two trees.

One of my fellow pastors at CCC set up the appointment. One of the cell leaders in this pastor's network was also in tow. Small talk ensued and then the cell leader began to unravel the following story. "Pastor Rob," she stated, "I am tired of covering up some things and I want to bring these things to the light. I want to experience tree of life living right now. For many years, I have tried to control my husband. I have tried everything to make him stop smoking marijuana. I also pray for God to work in his life. All of my efforts have been futile, I am very frustrated...but I know that God will one day change his heart. I have spent a great amount of time covering for him as various church folks have entered my house for cell gatherings. I was fearful that the church would find out. This fear would make me angry and I would lash out at him. I realized that I was eating off the wrong tree. I don't want to live like this anymore. My husband smokes grass and I have been highly unsuccessful in helping him break this habit. I have given God the full responsibility now to deal with this issue in his life. God must be the one to bring conviction to him and break this stronghold in his life. I wanted you to know this. If you desire for me to step down as a cell leader, then I will."

A broad smile filled my face. I responded, "I am so grateful to God for you. This is your husband's issue and in no way would I counsel you to step aside. I want you to know that credible sources who love you and your husband know about his habit. I know he smokes pot. I have known for many years. I love you and I love him. You should expect no change in my love for you or him. Thank you so much for sharing with me. You are now walking in the light and don't have to spend your time covering up his smoke!" My fellow pastor and I prayed for this leader and for her husband. As my friends left my office, I thanked God for soldiers in his army that walk in the light. *"If we walk in the light, as he is in the light, we have fellowship with one another, and the blood of Jesus, his Son, purifies us from all sin" (I John 1:7).*

I do not rejoice that a man I dearly love has been medicating his pain and hurt with marijuana. Frankly, sadness fills my heart concerning my friend's behavior, but I cannot ultimately change anyone. This is the work of God's Spirit. I interceded for my friend with a multitude of believers knowing that Jesus is the ultimate "need meeter" and the Spirit convicts bringing forth life. With great joy, I can report that God has freed this man of this addiction.

Love is the root and core motivational drive for tree of life living. The cry of the heart in this type of lifestyle is "Help me, God" versus self-help. A tree of life believer receives conviction from the Holy Spirit and conforms his/her life to him. Conviction is God reminding you and me that he has something better for us than what we are currently pursuing. Living from this life giving tree encourages, restores and stimulates the believer to be free. *"He has made us competent as ministers of a new covenant—not of the letter but of the Spirit; for the letter kills, but the Spirit gives life"* (2 *Corinthians 3:6).* Spiritual leaders become lifeguards, not umpires calculating the strikes in another person's life.

I have two observations for this tree of knowledge of good and evil mentality. First, we must willingly restore Jesus as the head of the church. The church is not "MY church," but "HIS church." A two headed body is a monster. Second, laws, regulations and rules have superceded God's Holy Spirit. The motivational root for this type of tree living is fear, control and manipulation. Condemnation replaces conviction. Discouragement, judgment and scrutiny reign. Life is quenched and the stench of death pervades.

Over nineteen hundred years ago, the Apostle John received an unveiling or revelation from Christ. In my opinion, there is no greater or more accurate description of the current state of today's church than what he records through the inspiration of the Holy Spirit in *Revelation 3:14-22.* In this passage, God displays his plan for the restoration of the church. During this holy encounter with John, Jesus Christ shares good news, bad news and the very best news one could discover.

The good news is that Jesus "knows" (*Rev. 3:15*) the current condition of his church. Underneath the facades, masks and stylish dresses and suits, Jesus knows. *"Jesus would not entrust himself to them, for he knew [and still knows] all men"* (*John 2:24*). At the pool of Bethesda, Jesus knew the lame man who had a reserved box seat at this vicinity for thirty eight years. He asks this man, "Do you want to get well?" Why did Jesus ask this man this question? My assumption is that Jesus also knew that this man found his identity in his sickness. Jesus knows about your church, the sickness. He desires to heal the lame legs of your church.

Not only does Jesus know, but he also loves (*Rev. 3:19*). His love for you and your church are not based on your performance or his personal feelings. Take a moment to ponder this thought—Jesus loves you. He knows you and he loves you. He knows your church and loves your church. Remember, he gave his very life for your church.

Further, Jesus pointedly and passionately shares with us some bad news. *"So, because you are lukewarm—neither hot nor cold—I am about to spit you out of my mouth" (Rev. 3:16).* Our passion and devotion for Christ has been exchanged for temporal pleasures, past times, and pursuits. In our own eyes, we are greater than he is. Our ways seem better, more appropriate. We have elevated our methodology, diverted his will, and compromised our hearts. We must remember that the man who becomes too big for his own britches will soon be exposed in the end! We expend a great deal of energy being in charge and staying in control. We live a facade. Pretending is the common cold of the Christian church.

Fortunately, Jesus shares the very best news we could ever hope for. *"Here I am! I stand at the door and knock. If anyone hears my voice and opens the door, I will come in and eat with him, and he with me" (Rev. 3:20).* Jesus is knocking on the door of your church. He desires to come in and eat with you from the tree of life. Will we respond to his voice? Will we *"listen to what the Spirit says to the churches?" (Rev. 3:22).* Jesus wants to exchange his guest badge and set up permanent residence in your church.

He knows, he loves, he corrects, and he invites you and me to his table of grace.

Chapter Four

"The Kiss, The Dance, The New Birth"

"Jesus Christ is the same yesterday and today and forever"
(Hebrews 13:8).

Mankind constantly changes. Our systems of rationale change like the seasons. Our fashions come and go—and come again. (Hold on to that old polyester suit! It may be hip in a few years.) Improved technology enables us to move from the very complex to the simple in lightning speed. We are connected to remote parts of the world through the click of a mouse. Some people are continually engaged in the search for truth, meaning, significance, happiness and purpose. Yes, the old adage rings true to this day: "How the times have changed."

Each year the staff at Beloit College in Wisconsin compiles a list of "current realities" for the faculty to grant awareness of the mind set of incoming freshman. The freshmen students who were born in 1982 (the year I graduated from high school) are characterized as follows: This group of students has no meaningful recollection of the Reagan Era and probably do not know he had ever been shot. They were prepubescent when the Persian Gulf War was waged. Black Monday (October 19, 1987) is as insignificant to them as the Great Depression. There has only been one Pope. They have no idea that Americans were ever held hostage in Iran. Bottle caps have always been screw off and plastic. The expression, "You sound like a broken record," means nothing to them. The Compact Disc was introduced when they were one-year old.

Most have never seen a television with only thirteen channels, nor have they seen a black and white television. They have always had cable. They have no idea what "BETA" is. They cannot fathom not having a remote control. They were born the year the Walkman was introduced by Sony. Jay Leno has always been on the Tonight Show. They don't know who Mork was or where he was from. They have never heard: "Where's the beef?" or "I'd walk a mile for a Camel," or "De plane, de plane." They do not care who shot J.R. and have no idea who J.R. is. There has always been MTV.

They have never seen Larry Bird play. They never took a swim and thought about Jaws. Kansas, Chicago, Boston, America and Alabama are places, not groups. They have always had an answering machine. They have no idea when or why Jordache jeans were cool. They can't imagine what hard contact lenses are. Popcorn has always been cooked in the microwave. Michael Jackson has always looked white!

I am feeling a tad old, how about you? Seriously, I am quite young. I was born in 1964 (you do the math). During my birth year, Nelson Mandela was sentenced to life in prison. Today's television classics including Bewitched, Gilligan's Island, The Munsters and The Addams Family debuted. Ten thousand screaming fans greeted the Beatles at JFK airport in New York prior to their performance on the Ed Sullivan show. Congress passed the Civil Rights Act prohibiting racial discrimination. Dr. Martin Luther King was the recipient of the Nobel Peace Prize. Health warnings were placed on cigarette packaging and advertisements for the first time. President Lyndon B. Johnson was elected in a landslide victory over Barry Goldwater. The Soviet leader, Khrushchev, fell from power and was ultimately replaced by Leonid Brezhnev.

The Ford Mustang was formally introduced with a base price of $2368.00. Sidney Poitier became the first black man to win an Oscar for best actor. Go-go girls populated discotheques. GI Joe was introduced by Hasbro. Pop Tarts were an instant success. China detonated its first atomic bomb. The average national price for a new home was $20,500.00, a quart of milk cost forty-eight cents, and the national per capita income was $2,663.00.

Indeed, times have changed! Only twenty years ago, there were 50,000 computers in the world. Now that many computers are being installed on a daily basis. Approximately 1,000 new products are introduced into America's supermarkets every month. In 1995, the Internet handled more mail than the 177 billion pieces that went through the U.S. Postal Service. The annual rate of growth for Internet traffic is 341,000%. In all of economic history, there is no technology that has grown faster than the World Wide Web. In 1969 only four primitive Web sites existed in the entire world. In 1990 there were 330,000. By the end of 1997 there were almost 20 million. It took 40 years for the radio to reach 50 million domestic users; it took 14 years for television to do that; and for the Internet, four years.[23] Yet, the majority of American people adhere to the following belief: "I do not like change!" Change will not go away; it will only get faster.

"Change-phobia" seems to be ingrained in our national heritage even though we delight in the improvements that change renders. For example, back in the 19th century numerous farmers denounced the steam locomotive for fear that the noise from this machine would impair their chickens from producing eggs and their cows from giving milk. Early Industrial Age critics warned that traveling in excess of 20 miles per hour for a lengthy period of time could cause insanity. Now don't miss this! The men and women who lived during this period averaged a life span of 35 years, the average marriage lasted 12 years, one-third of women died during child birth, and 50% of the children never reached the age of two.[24]

Holistically, let's take a look at change (where we have come from and where we are today). From the beginnings of recorded history through the seventeenth century (Premodernity), the universe was the playground of the gods or God. One's life was mystical and mysterious, beyond human control and could only be deciphered through supernatural terms. The signs of divine displeasure (natural disasters and disease) plagued mankind. Order and meaning were negotiated through a continual, cosmic poker game between outside forces and man.

Around 1600, a gradual and powerful shift occurred as human beings began to exert their own power to effect change in the world. God was removed from the throne of the cultural, theological, and philosophical domains. Man placed himself as the center of the universe. Science reigned supreme. Nothing is accepted unless it is first proven according to the dictates of science. Mankind regulated God (the referee) to the sidelines. As two and one-half centuries unfolded, science and rationalism triumph over religious faith and God is proclaimed dead."Modern" times have come and gone.

We are now told that we live in the Postmodern era. The term postmodern designates a 40-year transition from an Information Age to this current era. Defining adjectives for this period include "process-oriented," "pluralistic," "highly spiritual," "dynamic," "anti-dogmatic," and "nonrational." People are seeking a mystical unity with God. Truth is relative. Spiritual meaning for one's life is superior to proper belief. Extreme experiences with God and fellow travelers are sought after with immense vigor. Postmoderns love mystery.

I frequently travel from my country abode to the "big city" of Austin. On one such trip, I knew I was in for an exciting journey as a VW van darted around me on Sixth Street with a bumper sticker which read, "My karma just ran over your dogma." Traveling through the innards of this digital community, I saw the epitome of the postmodern man. He was entering an ornate, ten story office building. His garb is what first caught my eye. One of his knees was clearly visible through a horizontal tear in his Levis. His feet were shod with a pair of worn Reeboks. He donned a heavily starched pinpoint, button down, white oxford shirt which was covered with a blue, Polo sports coat. His necktie was perfectly tied, but hard on the eyes. He had preacher's hair—every lock in place and his black, heavy framed glasses rested prominently on his nose. Tucked under his left arm was an improperly folded newspaper as his left hand held an eloquent, brown leather attaché case. His entire head was tilted to the left to ensure that his cell phone would not detach from his left ear. He held a Starbucks cup in his right hand and clutched a street hockey stick which protruded from under his right armpit.

Lawrence Cunningham helps us to understand postmodern nuances as he writes, "I sit at my word processor (assembled here in the USA with chips made in Japan) in a pair of Levis sewn in Mexico while wearing a British brand of sneakers (Reeboks) which, a discreet tag informs, was manufactured in South Korea. For lunch, I will eat a salad made from vegetables grown in South Florida which were harvested by a vast army of migrant workers who are Hispanic or contract workers from the Caribbean"[25]

"Postmoderns can't draw a straight line. This is good news, as the mind does not work in linear but in spiralic fashion. Throw a ball and catch it: That's ministry in the modern world. Now let loose an inflated balloon and catch it: That's ministry in the postmodern world."[26] To say we live in interesting times would be an understatement. Most assuredly, we live in a dynamic time.

"As the Enlightenment has faded, postmodern people are increasingly suspicious of people and institutions that claim Authority, and they are increasingly dubious of Ultimate Explanations."[27] Prior to the Enlightenment, according to Martyn Atkins of England's Cliff College, people said,

> 'I belong, therefore I am.' Under the Enlightenment's influence, people said, 'I think, therefore I am.' Postmodern people now seem to be saying 'I feel, therefore I am,' or 'I shop, therefore I am,' or 'I look good, therefore I am,' or 'I disobey, therefore, I am,' or 'I doubt, therefore I am,' or 'I am, so what?'[28]

These alarming changes grant good news and bad news. The good news is that people are spiritually hungry. The church has an opportunity to fill this spiritual vacuum in the lives of millions of people. The bad news is twofold. First, the church lacks the spiritual power that is required to meet the cultural challenges. Second, the great majority of Americans believe the church to be highly irrelevant. "In an effort to appeal to the widest cultural audience, churches have elevated mind over heart, reason over faith, and activity over contemplation."[29] In simple terms, the church needs help...God inspired help.

The Kiss

The metaphor that rests in my mind concerning the church and culture[30] would be my first official kiss which proved to be an awkward experience. Let me explain. I was in sixth grade at Ft. Sam Houston Elementary in San Antonio, Texas. On Saturdays, a large pre-adolescent crowd would meet at the base theater for the matinee. One should not be fooled by the size of the crowd. The crowd was a simple collection of pairs—a guy and his girl—trying to act cool. I strolled up to the ticket window and said, "Two tickets please." I forked over a whole dollar bill and handed a ticket to my girl, Teri. Her hair was brown and fluffy shaped like a grown poodle. She wore wire framed glasses and heavy braces on her teeth. She was the cutest thing! We found our way to our seats and that's when she said to me, "Let's start with a kiss."

Trying not to look shocked for fear I might blow my cover as an "experienced" sixth grader, I turned my face toward her and tilted my head. She mirrored my actions and we finally reached alignment for a quick kiss on the lips. I was quite certain that Teri could hear my pounding heart. We held hands. About midway through the movie, she turned to me and posed a question. "Robby (that was my name back then), would you please let go of my hand so I can eat my peanut butter sandwich my mother fixed for me?" I obliged her request, but thought her to be quite odd at this point. The movie soon ended. We said goodbye. Two days later on the playground during recess, we decided not "to go" with each other anymore. I felt free from her shackles. Boy, she was a high maintenance individual.

Awkward times (like this first kiss) are uniquely etched into my memory. I have a hunch that I tilted my head three or four times, burning up precious time as I tried to zero in on Teri's small, thin lips. As I reflect upon this klutzy kiss, I don't remember thinking, "Maybe I shouldn't kiss this girl." This thought never occurred to me. She suggested we kiss, and I gratified her desire.

As the church tilts her face to align herself with culture, a troublesome and touchy predicament is produced. Should the church kiss the culture? Is the culture willing to be preciously pecked by the church? Who is watching the tilting and alignment of our lips? Do we kiss with our eyes wide open or forcefully shut? What will others think if we choose to kiss this culture?

A few scriptures might shed some light on this present day matinee between the church and culture. The most quoted and well known scriptural passage (by Christians and not-yet believers) is *"For God so loved the world that he gave his one and only son, that whoever believes in him should not perish but have eternal life" (John 3:16).* God is our model, and his motive for giving us Jesus is his love. Look at the measure of God's love for the world. He gave us his *one and only* son. Have we forgotten that God loves the world? Let's consider the very next verse which reads, *"For God did not send his Son into the world to condemn the world, but to save the world through him."* My impression is that the world feels condemned by the church. Wait a minute, now! Is not Jesus the head of the church? Have we as God's people lost our passion to kiss culture? By the way, "the type of kissing that I am writing about goes beyond lip service to life service."[31]

For too long the church has been fearful of the culture and blatantly proclaimed the "world" to be evil. Yet, God is in culture and created the world. God loves the world and *perfect love casts out fear.* We need not fear the arts, movies, dance, music, drama....or people. Here's why. *"In all these things we are more than conquerors through him who loved us" (Romans 8:37).* Consider the example of Daniel.

Daniel was taken captive by King Nebuchadnezzar of Babylon and *"taught the language and literature of the Babylonians" (Daniel 1:4b).*

> This must have included not only a mastery of spoken Chaldean but also Akkadian, the official, literary language of Babylon from the days of Hammurabi and before.... Babylonian religion had always required a thorough knowledge of Sumerian literature—religious, magical, astrological and scientific.... Thus they [Daniel and his friends] prepared themselves for the final examinations in all kinds of literature and learning.[32]

Daniel and his comrades were immersed in the culture of the

Babylonians—the evil empire. *Daniel 1:20* states, *"In every matter of wisdom and understanding about which the king questioned them, he found them ten times better than all the magicians and enchanters in his whole kingdom."* If God had not been on Daniel's side, then he would have easily become a pagan priest. But, Daniel did not bow down to the Babylonian's god and he *"resolved not to defile himself with the royal food and wine" (Daniel 1:8).* He aced the king's exam and honored God. He was successful in engaging culture without fear. Of course, his God given ability to interpret dreams did not hurt God's purpose in his young life! Because of his spiritual fortitude, Daniel later held a prominent position under the Persian ruler, Cyrus.

Jesus prayed, *"Holy Father, protect them by the power of your name—the name you gave me—so that they may be one as we are one...My prayer is not that you take them out of the world but that you protect them from the evil one. They are not of the world, even as I am not of it. Sanctify them by the truth; your word is truth. As you sent me into the world, I have sent them into the world" (John 17:11, 15-18).* The people of God are sent as salt, light and leaven into the world protected by the name of Jesus. We need not fear kissing this culture as we engage those for whom Christ died.

The Dance

A few months before my wedding to Susan in December, 1986, I was in need of some desperate help. My bride to be and I desired for our wedding reception to be a time of great celebration. We wanted to literally dance the night away. The problem was that I was a lousy dancer. "Not to worry," Susan assured me, "We'll sign up for dance lessons!" This seemed like a logical answer to my dilemma.

I struggled at first with "leading" Susan for she is actually a very good dancer. The dance lessons were fun, and I really thought I was making outstanding progress. However, our dance instructor was not pleased with my style. She encouraged me to "loosen up" and "go with the flow of the music." "You're too tight, Rob," she shouted over the loud music, "Relax, have some fun." I was having fun, but I apparently was not her favorite pupil. At the end of one session she encouraged me to return the next week with a "few drinks" under my belt. As the weeks progressed, my confidence level increased and I was ready for my dance debut.

The wedding was marvelous and we made our way to the town's Civic Center for the wedding reception. I was cautiously optimistic that I could fake my way through the first dance of the evening with my new bride precisely emulating Fred Astaire. The big time came and I twirled my girl around a few times. The guests graciously clapped and the celebration began. Was I really that great or were people just being kind?

Immediately, a deacon from the Baptist church where I was employed as youth pastor approached me. "Rob," he stated, "Tonight you were an excellent witness for Christ." I beamed from ear to ear. He continued, "You're a lousy dancer and Christ is exalted." This was not the kind of affirmation I hoped for. Apparently, the dance lessons were a big waste of money! I'd better stick with preachin' and leave the two-step to my members. I do long, however, to be excellent in both pursuits.

Jesus stated, *"To what, then, can I compare the people of this generation? What are they like? They are like children sitting in the marketplace and calling out to each other: 'We played the flute for you, and you did not dance; we sang a dirge, and you did not cry.'"* (*Luke 7:31-32*). Can today's church dance with this postmodern culture? Do we have two left feet? Do we spend a lot of money in preparation for the big dance only to fall short of the eventual goal? Are we lousy dancers? Are we willing to let God lead us in a new dance with Him?

Joey is a young man who has experienced some rough years. He is known as the "dancer," "twirler," or "bouncer" at Cypress Creek Church. As we worship God, his passion for God cannot be contained and he begins to dance, twirl, and bounce around with great zeal and sincerity. He loves to worship God. I love to watch Joey worship God.

A recent guest to CCC was not real thrilled about Joey's beautiful expression to God. In a phone conversation with Pastor Jim, she asked, "Why didn't some adult in leadership tell that kid to sit down and stop him from dancing and twirling around?" Jim kindly explained that Joey had experienced a dramatic conversion to Christ and we appreciated his passion. Jim said, "We would rather have our kids dance to the Lord than dance at some honky-tonk." He further explained that this guest should not expect anyone in leadership to stifle Joey's dancing and twirling. He ended the conversation with a suggestion to this guest (and her family) to investigate some areas churches that worshiped God through different means.

This guest might learn something by reading one of A.A. Milne's *"Winnie the Pooh and Tigger Too"* classics. I recently viewed the same story with my four-year-old (Kayley) during her pre-nap preparation. In the story, Mr. Rabbit is disgusted with Tigger's obnoxious and consistent bounce. Tigger bounces on Mr. Rabbit, Pooh, Roo, Christopher Robin, and Piglet throughout the story. Tigger bounces everywhere he goes. Mr. Rabbit is irritated by Tigger and eventually develops a strategy with the help of the other characters to fix Tigger once and for all. At the end of the story, Tigger finds himself in a precarious place, stuck in a tree and filled with fear. As the other characters assemble at the base of the tree, Tigger pronounces, "I will never bounce again if you get me down from here." Mr. Rabbit is delighted and makes certain that everyone present hears Tigger's promise. A successful strategy is produced which allows Tigger to return to flat land. Mr. Rabbit reminds Tigger of his promise and holds him to it. Sadly and slothfully, Tigger walks away with his head down and no bounce to his step. He looks miserable and the other characters realize that they don't appreciate the "new" Tigger. Collectively, the characters release Tigger from his promise and immediately with immense glee and delight he bounces upon—you guessed it—Mr. Rabbit! The story teaches us about our human nature to control and the demands we place upon others to act in accordance with who we are.

"Let them praise his name with dancing!" (Psalm 149:3a). Are we willing to dance with God? Both of my daughters love to dance to the Lord. Recently, my daughter Kayley, inserted her favorite worship CD into the jambox in our living room and waited for the tunes to begin. I watched her from a reclined position in my leather recliner. The music began and she turned to me and stated, "Dance with me, Daddy." Now, I have already confessed to being a lousy

dancer, but how could I resist this earnest plea from my youngest daughter? I looked around the general area to see if my wife and oldest daughter were in sight. They were not. I didn't totally want to make a fool out of myself. I lifted my body from my chair and began to dance with Kayley. Her radiant smile and steady giggle captured my heart and dismantled my human apprehension. Soon, the living room was transformed into a Worship Center and the whole family joined in.

God, our Daddy, is asking his children, "Will you dance with me?" I am speaking more of a dance of the heart than a dance with our bodies. The new dance that God is calling his church to is a dance that presents a bonded and braided band of Christ's body, his bride. Jesus, the groom, is leading his bride. An accomplished instructor, a wedding reception guest, and a worship spectator may still critique the fluidity, style and movement of the new dance. But the fact remains, God is calling his people to step up and out with him.

The New Birth

The most exhilarating experience of my life was to watch (and participate in) the birth of my oldest daughter, Taylor. My very pregnant wife was two weeks overdue. It was summer in Texas and we were ready for something to give. The doctor decided to induce labor and on August 16, 1989 at 7:30 A.M. we headed from Wimberley to New Braunfels via Purgatory Road in our '83 Cutlass Supreme. I pondered the thought of performing an emergency delivery utilizing the knowledge gained in the La Maze birthing classes. As my eyes swept across my wife's glowing face, my nervousness about the journey to the hospital was put to rest. She was meticulously painting her fingernails!

We arrived without incident if you don't consider a few blemishes on one of Susan's nails due to the bump in the road. We settled into the birthing suite and the nurse began to insert an IV in Susan's arm. I left the room. Have I mentioned my weak stomach? A few hours later, labor ensued. Back labor hit my lovely blonde with a vengeance. I continually dropped ice chips into her mouth and "coached" her employing the breathing techniques we learned in La Maze. By the way, I will go to my grave knowing in my heart of hearts that La Maze is best translated, "brain washing." After twenty-eight hours of labor (and too much TV), our new baby came into the world.

In my glee as tears streamed down my face, I shouted out, "It's a boy! It's a boy!" "No," Dr. Ousley kindly stated, "That's the umbilical cord, Rob. You're the father of a beautiful baby girl." I didn't do real well in Human Anatomy class in Jr. High! I shouted again, "It's a girl, Susan. It's a girl."

I anticipated the scene to be filled with commotion as the doctor and the attending nurses scurried about the delivery room passing surgical instruments to one another with great haste. I further anticipated that my little angel would wail continually proclaiming her entrance into the world. None of these scenarios played out. The medical folks in the room were serene and collected. Taylor didn't even test out her healthy set of lungs (yet!). Dr. Ousley placed the baby into Susan's arms and he and the attending staff left the room. I wrapped my arms around Susan and Taylor, cried tears of joy, and prayed a prayer of thanksgiving. The room was still, silent...and I was exhausted feeling like I had been at a Jr. High lock-in. What a miracle...new birth!

God believes in new birth! There is no greater miracle than when the supernatural touches the natural. When God touches the heart of man. He loves the new birth of the soul. He loves new birth in his church.

"Forget the former things; do not dwell on the past. See, I am doing a new thing! Now it springs up; do you not perceive it?" (Isaiah 43:18-19). God is raising up a highly visible community of faith shaped by a story of how God is with us that follows the way of Jesus and is fully integrated into its surrounding culture. This community of faith is the church. Will this church kiss a culture which God created and loves? Will this church dance a new dance following his lead? Will this church experience a new and fresh birth of his Spirit?

PART TWO:

OUR STORY
"LEARNING THE DANCE STEPS TOGETHER"

Chapter Five

"Leaders Who Look Like Jesus"
(Empowering Leadership)

YOU GOTTA DANCE...

The *Waltz* continues to be one of the most popular dances the world over. With long sweeping movements, constant rotating and stylish poses, the Waltz is a romantic dance that commands attention. It takes a bit more concentration to learn at first, but the pay off is great. The reason for this is at first you have to learn to navigate the floor without playing bumper cars. That's the tough part. After you get past the basics, the patterns and moves start to become easier to grasp.

As a leader, if you are waltzing merely to call attention to yourself, then the trials of church life will eventually consume you. A leader who refuses to be the lone star of the dance floor will concentrate on empowering others—navigating the challenges, grabbing hold of God's dancing hand and moving with the Spirit—in the context of team ministry. This is the beautiful and graceful dance of leadership.

DANCE WITH ME, DADDY...

Simple instruments such as the flute were used in the *Dance of Anointing* to usher in the presence of the Lord.

"You [Samuel] will go to Gibeah of God, where there is a Philistine outpost. As you approach the town, you will meet a procession of prophets coming down from the high place with lyres, tambourines, flutes and harps being played before them, and they will be prophesying. **The Spirit of the Lord will come upon you in power,** *and you will prophesy with them; and you will be changed into a different person. Once these signs are fulfilled, do whatever your hand finds to do, for God is with you"* (I Samuel 10:5-7).

"And all the people went up after him [Solomon], **playing flutes and rejoicing greatly,** *so that the ground shook with the sound"* (I Kings 1:40).

INTRODUCTION
(by Jennifer Ruiz, CCC Children's Network Pastor)

It is essential to entrust people to lead out in a body of believers to encourage health and growth. One person can effectively shepherd just so many followers. Jesus is our model: He appointed 12 disciples; pouring into their lives to spread the good news to the nations. In turn, the twelve disciples chose others to assist them. As a result of this model of empowerment, the world has been changed. Leaders of healthy and growing churches focus on empowering other Christians for ministry. Everyone is called by God; some listen and obey, and some turn away. Everyone is a potential leader to carry on the good news to all who will listen. It is not up to us to determine who will be God's spokesperson, this is the job of the creator. It took many years for me to realize this.

In the early years of Cypress Creek Church, I served as a volunteer in the children's cell network. I was self reliant and independent relying on my own power to pull off the assorted tasks of ministry. I acted as if I did not need others to help me. Further, I did not accept help from others. Here's the bottom line: I was a self-indulged rascal not wanting anyone but myself to get the glory of a successful ministry.

Pastor Rob continued to motivate me through all the rough spots, giving me a chance to learn through my own mistakes. Needless to say, I was overwhelmed even in the simplest of tasks. I was being pressed to surrender many of my duties to a capable willing team of leaders. Today, I'm very thankful for the leadership in the children's cell network and their humble attitude.

As I look back over the years, God entrusted me with the lives of children and leaders. Pastor Rob modeled to me what empowerment was all about. Yes, it has been a scary ride, but quite adventurous. Along the way, one scripture that has encouraged me is *Matthew 24:45-47* which states, *"Who then is the faithful and wise servant, whom the master has put in charge of the servants in his household to give them food at the proper time? It will be good for that servant whose master finds him doing so when he returns. I tell you the truth, he will put him in charge of all his possessions."*

In a recent conversation with a pastor friend, I found myself verbally enthusiastic about empowering others for ministry. I got really stirred up and stated (maybe even shouted) at my second office (Cypress Creek Café), "We must reform the clergy!" The flow of the conversation was going quite well until my wise friend asked the following question: "Who do we think we are as leaders 'empowering' others for ministry?" The question fazed me for a minute. I thought, "This is what I know. This is my passion—to release others into ministry." Yet, a nagging, continual pull of my heart brought me back to the original question. "Who do you think you are, Campbell, empowering others for ministry?" This question swirled within my mind and heart. I know that I am nothing apart from God. I know that I am a very simple man. I know that I have no power except through the Spirit of God. I know who ultimately empowers others for ministry. So, what is my role?

After a few days of wrestling with this question, I decided to go to the source—the manual for life—God's word. I found that Jesus is the one who is full of the Spirit's power (*Luke 4:14*). This power enabled Him to heal the sick (*Luke 5:17*). Further, Jesus extends His power to His disciples. *"When Jesus had called the Twelve together, he gave them **power** and authority to drive out all demons and to cure diseases, and he sent them out to preach the kingdom of God and to heal the sick (Luke 9:1-2)."* He further states to his disciples, *"I have given you authority to trample on snakes and scorpions and to overcome all the **power** of the enemy; nothing will harm you. However, do not rejoice that the spirits submit to you, but rejoice that your names are written in heaven." (Luke 10:19-20).* Before His ascension into Heaven Jesus said, *"I am going to send you what my Father has promised; but stay in the city until you have been clothed with **power** from on high" (Luke 24:49).*

You see, my friend, just as Jesus ministered in the **power** of the Spirit, we too are granted, through Christ, this same **power**. In essence, we empower no one, but Christ empowers us through the Spirit of God. *"But you will receive **power** when the Holy Spirit comes on you; and you will be my witnesses in Jerusalem, and in all Judea and Samaria, and to the ends of the earth" (Acts 1:8).*

Paul testified, *"I became a servant of this gospel by the gift of God's grace given me through the working of his **power**" (Ephesians 3:7).* Paul's commandment to the church of Ephesus is to *"be strong in the Lord and in his mighty **power**" (Ephesians 6:10).* God granted to every believer the **power** of the Spirit (*2 Timothy 1:7*). Further, God grants this promise: *"His divine **power** has given us everything we need for life and godliness through our knowledge of him who called us by his own glory and goodness. Through these he has given us his very great and precious promises, so that through them you may participate in the divine nature and escape the corruption in the world caused by evil desires" (2 Peter 1:3).*

Let me recap by asking two key questions. Who empowers others for ministry? What is my role as a spiritual leader in this empowerment process? First, Jesus is full of the Spirit of God—His source for power. He empowers you for ministry through His Spirit. Next, Jesus desires to release His power to his followers. Finally, as a leader I must follow the example of Jesus and be a conduit of God's power in the lives of others to release them for ministry. Therefore, as a pastor, God uses me to empower others for ministry. This reality has nothing to do with my own power, but God's power through me as Jesus exemplified in His own earthly ministry.

We see this impartation of leadership ability throughout the scriptures. *"The Lord took some of the spirit that was upon Moses and put it upon the seventy elders, and they shall bear the burden of the people with you, that you may not bear it alone" (Numbers 11:17).* As Moses prepared to relinquish his leadership role with the people of Israel, he said of Joshua (his successor), *"Take Joshua, the son of Nun, a man in whom is the spirit, and lay your hand upon him. Give him some of your authority so the whole Israelite community will obey him" (Numbers 27:18, 20).* Be reminded of how David was selected by God to rule Israel. *"Then Samuel took the horn of oil, and anointed him in the midst of his brothers; and the Spirit of the Lord came mightily upon David from that day forward" (I Samuel 16:33).*

If you are still wrestling with your role in this process, then consider the following relationships of empowerment found in scriptures: King Artaxerxes and Nehemiah, Elijah and Elishah, Jesus and his twelve, Jesus and the seventy, Barnabas and Saul (Didn't the 'son of encouragement' partner with God in empowering this former murderer of Christians?), Paul and Silas, Barnabas and John Mark, Paul and Timothy.

There are many more examples, but let's focus on you. Who partnered with God in empowering you to minister? Who believed in you? Who encouraged you? Who mentored you in your abilities, spiritual gifts and talents? Who took the time to listen to the dream that God put in your heart? Now, are you God's conduit in empowering others? Or, are you all God needs in your field or area to do the work of ministry? How is God using you in empowering others for ministry?

Christian Schwarz writes, "Leaders of growing churches concentrate on empowering other Christians for ministry. They do not use lay workers as 'helpers' in attaining their own goals and fulfilling their own visions. Rather, they invert the pyramid of authority so that the leader assists Christians to attain the spiritual potential God has for them."[33] M. Scott Peck wrote in *A World Waiting to be Born:* "Increasingly, the civil leader or manager begins to sense that the power of her position is not hers. It is not her possession; it is not hers to possess. The power belongs to God, and the proper role of the civil leader is merely to be a conduit and to steward that power as God's agent. Merely! What a paradox! To exercise temporal power with civility is to undertake a role of great glory, and it can only be undertaken with genuine humility."[34] A spiritual leader saturated with the humility of Christ releases others for ministry so that God's power may be extended.

The Leadership House (at the University of South Florida) dedicated to understanding empowering others for leadership, uses the goose as its mascot. Let me explain this curious selection.

Geese, of course, fly in a 'V' formation for several reasons. By flying together, they provide an uplift that makes them more efficient as a group. They encourage each other vocally. They take turns flying "point" so that the leader doesn't wear down. And when a goose gets sick or wounded, two geese drop out of formation and follow it down to help and protect it. They stay with the goose until it is either able to fly again or dies. Only then do they launch out on their own. [This teaches us] that people who share a common direction and sense of community can get where they are going quicker and easier. It is a good idea to take turns doing the difficult tasks and sharing leadership; interdependency is important.[35]

One business leader who apparently embraces this 'V' formation among the people she leads is Meg Whitman, the chief executive of eBay. Ms. Whitman was traveling in Japan the day of the terrorist attacks upon America (9-11-01). Flowing with eBay's environment and mentality of empowerment, the executive leadership team (in the absence of Whitman and Brian Swette, the chief operating officer, who was in Florida), stepped to the plate. The team established three priorities: 1. Determine if all 2,500 employees were alive and well (they were), 2. Secure the eBay web site (they did), and 3. Create a way for the organization to support the impending relief effort which led to the development of eBay's relief initiative, "Auction for America." "By the time I was able to call in from Japan," said Ms. Whitman, "Our team was already thinking about and acting on the big issues."[36]

This 'V' modality of leadership, releasing others through empowerment, is not the norm in churches today. Indeed, the church has fallen into a non-Biblical power play between professional clergy and laity. Pastors have falsely concluded that "if the work is going to get done, then I'm going to have to do it." The "non-professionals" throw a few coins or bills in the plate as a tip to God so that the hired gun(s) can handle the weddings, funerals, counseling, lawn maintenance, gardening, preaching, teaching, and make sure that the toilets are working and ready for Sunday's service. William Brown boldly states, "The reversion to an "official" priesthood of ministry...cast the laity chiefly into the role of hearers of the Law and spectators of the mysterious tableau of the sacrifices. This passive role in worship became once more the normal experience of the people of God as the church developed."[37]

Brilliant writer, leader, and historian Leonard Sweet flings an arrow at the heart of this issue. "It is now time," Sweet writes, "to disestablish the clergy in the church once and for all. Postmodern culture is an 'age of participation,' an 'age of access.' The modern world was an 'age of representation,' its goal to 'represent' to the people 'the best that has been thought and said.' The postmodern world is a karaoke world."[38] Another arrow might be hurled in the direction of the laity as a rebuke for falling into such lethargy. Statistically, typical church participation among the laity is as follows: 66% are observers, 6% are teachers, 4% are leaders, and the remaining 24% are categorized as "other."[39]

Let's return to Jesus, our example, the one who demonstrated empowering others for ministry. *"Jesus knew that the Father had put all things under his **power**, and that he had come from God and was returning to God; so he got up from the meal, took off his outer clothing, and wrapped a towel around his waist. After that, he poured water into a basin and began to wash his disciples' feet, drying them [the disciples] with the towel that was wrapped around him"* (*John 13:3-5*). "Unbelievable," you might say. Yes, Jesus in his power *stooped* and washed the smelly, dirty feet of his disciples. He exemplifies the servant leader through this spiritual parody of *power* and *service*. "You want to lead? Be willing to serve. The more you serve, the more humble you become, the more confident you can be. Appointed to lead means anointed to serve, means ability to listen, to learn, to admit mistakes, to deny yourself, to let others get the credit."[40]

I believe that many Christians are angry concerning the minimization of their spiritual gifts and the lack of a church based outlet for ministry. In their mind, the professional clergy is hogging the ministry of the church. The clergy is paralyzed in fear concerning releasing God's people to minister. This posture is foreign to the model of Christ. Maybe the clergy really believes that they can do the work of the ministry in a far superior way without the aid of the laity. (By the way, please know that I detest these terms "clergy" and "laity," but I am using them in order that I might effectively communicate). Maybe pastors are uncomfortable with releasing and empowering others for the ministry for many reasons including control, poor self-esteem, insecurity, pride and ignorance. Research shows that the lack of intentional empowerment by the church's key leader has driven away literally a million Christians who are gifted leaders.[41]

Gail Neal is making significant shifts at the Synod of Mid-America, Presbyterian Church (USA) in Overland Park, Kansas where he serves. The first shift is one of trust. He contends, "For too long the Bible has been the purview of the clergy. Laity have relied upon ordained ministers to interpret the Biblical faith for them and to them. Christians need to learn to end their dependence upon the clergy in order to trust the presence and power of the God of Abraham, Isaac, and Jacob, the God of Mary Magdalene,

Martha, and Priscilla. In this new world it is imperative that the people themselves possess the Biblical knowledge and interpretation skills which will enable them to live faithfully within culture that has forsaken God."[42]

Neal's second shift concerns church leadership. "No longer will the clergy be the main link between the church and the unchurched. The focus of the ordained ministry will shift instead to equipping the saints to serve God on the home mission field of daily life, for it is they who will be the primary witnesses to the love of God in Christ Jesus our Lord."[43] Can other pastors make similar shifts to release and empower?

Blatantly honest and consistently brash radio talk show host, Dr. Laura Schlessinger, expressed her views of the clergy on *NBC's Meet the Press*. "I think the clergy—with all due respect—have become more like camp counselors than leaders. What they're doing is saying, 'I want the people to come back next week. You can't challenge them too much, can't ask them too much, can't tell them that religion demands something of them.' God demands something of you." Do you agree with Dr. Laura's assertion leveled at clergy? Are you more of a camp counselor or a leader? What is a leader anyway? Glad you asked.

The Christian community has been plastered with explanations of what a leader does, looks like, says, and more. "Leadership is modeling." "Leadership is influence." "Do you think you're a leader? Look over your shoulder. Is anyone following you or are you merely taking a walk?" While these explanations have been somewhat helpful to me in my own ministry, I have a need to drill down a little deeper and extract the heart of leadership in the context of empowering others for ministry. In essence, we have already done this by seeing the servant leadership style of Jesus.

What is leadership? There are four definitions that stir me. I give to you these four definitions because the task of defining an effective leader is gargantuan.

- "Leadership is a dynamic process in which a man or woman with God-given capacity influences a specific group of God's people toward His purposes for the group."[44]

- "Leadership occurs any time one attempts to influence the behavior of an individual or group, regardless of reason."[45]

- "The signs of outstanding leadership appear primarily among the followers. Are they reaching their potential? Are they learning?"[46]

- "An effective leader is one who is called by God to lead, possesses the character of a person of God, and demonstrates a group of competencies that result in leadership. A leader implements the gift and ability to lead by motivating, mobilizing, resourcing and directing people to pursue a jointly shared vision from God."[47]

These definitions inspire me, but let's put them on the bookshelf for a moment and consider what obstacles we ultimately must face as leaders. (For one of the best resources concerning leadership rooted in character, see *The Ascent of a Leader,* San Francisco, CA: Josey Bass Publishers, 1999.)

In July 1994, Chuck Swindoll spoke at the Promise Keepers Leadership Conference in Boulder, Colorado. As he stepped to the podium, he looked intently from left to right at the thousands who had gathered for this event. I was one of those in attendance, seated in the very front row next to Coach McCartney. Swindoll said, "Pastors, lighten up...lighten up!" I loved his admonishment for I have always believed that pastors are too tight, serious, posturing themselves to be more important than they really are. The place filled with laughter and Chuck continued. This masterful communicator cited the dirty dozen obstacles to leadership. They are as follows: Authoritarianism, Exclusiveness, Greed, Hypocrisy, Sensuality, Prejudice, Pride, Rationalization, Manipulation, Secrecy, Unaccountability, and Traditionalism. As he rattled off this deplorable, dirty dozen list, conviction fell on me. I sensed God saying to me, "Rob, leadership is a big deal. Continually clothe yourself in me."

Returning to the leadership definitions, let me pluck out three overarching themes that I'm sure are obvious to you. First, a leader sees the way (vision). Second, fellow team members and followers are essential for the journey (mission). Finally, leaders must be passionate about people for relationships are the key to any successful quest (passion). *Ecclesiastes 4:12* states, *"A cord of three strands is not quickly broken."* Let me introduce you to the three strands of an effective leader: vision, mission and passion.

Vision

I am a visionary leader. I love to dream dreams with God and my fellow team members. There are many wonderful definitions for vision. I personally like this one: Vision is a God inspired strategic understanding of a different future. *"He is able to do exceeding abundantly beyond all that we ask or think according to his power that works within us"* (Ephesians 3:20). *"Forget the former things; do not dwell on the past. See, I am doing a new thing! Now it springs up; do you not perceive it? I am making a way in the desert and streams in the wasteland"* (Isaiah 43:18-19). *"Where there is no vision, the people perish"* (Proverbs 29:18). These visionary scriptures light my fire. I love to see God do a new thing. I love change. I love for God to pull back the curtain of His future and give me a glimpse of what is ahead. Vision is hearing and seeing God's dream before it is a reality. When you think of vision, consider the word "seeing."

Mission

I love the mission of the vision. Being on mission involves the actual carrying out of the God-given task which requires diligence and commitment. Mission, unlike the initial vision, is not carried out by one individual. It is a "body" or team effort. In the scriptures, we find a strong, dedicated leader of the people of God—his name is Moses. Moses was a brilliant man, educated in all the wisdom of the Egyptians (*Acts 7:22*). When we think of Moses, we recall God using him to part the Red Sea. We remember the challenges presented to him by his own people as they wandered through the wilderness. We think of his mentoring abilities with certain proteges like Joshua. There were times, however, when Moses needed others to experience God's power. Here are three examples.

First, Moses was called by God to speak with the Egyptian Pharaoh and lead God's people to liberty. His response to the Lord may ring of familiarity to you. *"O Lord, I have never been eloquent,"* he said. *"I am slow of speech and tongue" (Exodus 4:10).* Here, Moses is expressing to God his lack of confidence and power. How does God respond? God instructs Moses to take his brother, Aaron, with him to speak with the Pharaoh. In essence, God said to Moses, "Okay, my chosen leader, look around you— who is best qualified on your team to deliver the goods when you meet with Pharaoh? If you need some help from me, look to your brother, Aaron. He is my gift to you."

The second episode illustrating Moses' need for others occurs during Israel's battle with the Amalekites. In *Exodus 17:10-13* we read, *"Moses, Aaron and Hur went to the top of the hill. As long as Moses held up his hands, the Israelites were winning, but whenever he lowered his hands, the Amalekites were winning. When Moses' hands grew tired, they took a stone and put it under him and he sat on it. Aaron and Hur held his hands up—one on one side, one on the other—so that his hands remained steady till sunset. So Joshua overcame the Amalekite army."*

Finally, in *Exodus 18* we find a very tired and weary leader. Moses was serving the people as judge from morning till evening. Enter Jethro, Moses' father-in-law. Jethro is being used of God as he says to Moses, *"You and these people who come to you will only wear yourselves out. The work is too heavy for you; you cannot handle it alone" (Exodus 18:18).* Jethro further advises Moses to select capable people who would serve as judges over thousands, hundreds, fifties and tens, leaving only the most difficult cases to Moses.

Please notice that in all three cases cited above—God provided the power for Moses to be an effective leader. God sent Moses other people—his team members. Now, don't miss Moses' response to these three scenarios in his life. He *received* his team members as a gift from God. This reception of help is rooted in humility. Moses' humility to receive other team members to assist him on God's given mission was a source of power, keeping him fresh, focused and effective.

Consider Jesus. Jesus knew his mission. *"My food,"* said Jesus, *"is to do the will of him who sent me and to finish his work" (John 4:34).* In the next verse, Jesus rallies his team by saying, *"I tell you, open your eyes and look at the fields! They are ripe for harvest."* Jesus knew his mission and he encouraged others to join him. This mission of the harvest burned in the soul of Jesus. This mission also led him to the cross and cost him his life. *"When he had received the drink, Jesus said, 'It is finished.' With that, he bowed his head and gave up his spirit" (John 19:30).* Would you say that Jesus was committed to his Father's mission for his life? What is God's tailored made mission for you? What is God asking you to accomplish that burns in your soul? Notice that mission is connected to the vision. When you think of mission, consider the word "doing."

Passion

The final strand of a successful leader is passion. Those with passion have a servant's heart and a burning desire to pursue God. Jesus was a passionate person. Watch his passion and zeal displayed in the following scenario. *"When it was almost time for the Jewish Passover, Jesus went up to Jerusalem. In the temple courts he found men selling cattle, sheep and doves, and others sitting at tables exchanging money. So he made a whip out of cords, and drove all from the temple area, both sheep and cattle; he scattered the coins of the money changers and overturned their tables. To those who sold doves he said, 'Get these out of here! How dare you turn my Father's house into a market!' " (John 2:13-16).* Jesus was passionate about the temple which he wanted to protect as a house of prayer.

Passion is our personal motivation that overflows into the lives of others. Yes, passion is contagious. The passion of Paul and Silas is evident as they are accused of *"turning the world upside down" (Acts 17:6)* for the gospel of Christ. You will know passion when the pain is greater than the reward. Antoine de Saint Exupery is noted for saying, "If you want to build a ship, don't drum up the men to gather wood, divide the work, and give orders. Instead, teach them to yearn for the vast and endless sea." We are looking for men and women who have a passion for the sea of the harvest. When you think of passion, consider the word "feeling."

Vision (seeing), mission (doing), and passion (feeling) are commendable and necessary traits for an effective leader. Each strand is essential as you serve others. For example, if you lack mission and passion, then chances are strong you will jump from project to project. Further, if you have strong strands of passion and mission but lack vision, then you will give yourself to too small a task. Finally, if you lack passion but have immense vision and mission strands, then you will not have the heart to inspire others and the vision will become dry and laborious.

Spiritual leadership is a high calling and can be filled with great joy and/or immense pain. A great deal is expected from key leaders. These expectations can become burdensome as a pastor tries to become all things to all people. Can you guess which group is "the single most occupationally frustrated professionals in America?" That's right—you nailed it! The answer is pastors.[48] Pastors are in need of help and help is available as they intentionally and deliberately empower others for ministry. Pastors must consistently be on the lookout for emerging leaders. "This means you may get less done in the present, but you will actually accomplish far more in the future by pouring your life into the people who can carry on those things that are nearest and dearest to your heart."[49]

Throughout the scriptures, God reveals vision to an individual person (Abraham, Noah, Moses, Paul, etc.). At the same time, God is into teams to walk and live in mission with one another to fulfill a dream from the heart of God. Overall, pastors are lousy at involving others in the mission of the vision. Founder of Leadership Network and author, Bob Buford, suggests, "I have never done anything important outside the context of team. I think God must laugh at the seeming independence of us human beings who have such a tendency toward hubris and self-sufficiency."[50] Albert Einstein is noted for this confession of teamness, "A hundred times every day I remind myself that my inner and outer life depend on the labors of other men, living and dead, and that I must exert myself in order to give in the same measure as I have received and am still receiving."

If you are the key leader in your ministry or church, then God desires for you to have a team. Teams work best when there is a collective admission that each member needs the others, not just to pursue the vision or trek together on a mission, but to experience personal fulfillment.

"If you study the leaders described in the Bible you soon discover that every great leader called by God worked with a strong team of ministry associates. The fact that churches are now embracing a leader-led, multiple-person, team-based ministry is exciting and certainly bodes well for the future of the American Church."[51] It is interesting to note that in a recent research study conducted by the Barna Research Group only 5% of senior pastors (or pastoral team leaders) identified "leadership" as one of their spiritual gifts. Further, 69% of the same individuals surveyed cited "preaching/teaching" as their primary spiritual gift.[52] For a pastor who is not gifted in leadership to submit to another person on his team to be the primary leader is not a disgrace. In fact, this very act is rooted in humility, sacrifice, and service. If one lacks the gift of leadership, then this same individual can still be the primary teacher in the church. However, a need for leadership in the church must be filled by a fellow team member. As a reminder, when we stay in our giftedness we experience fruitfulness and fulfillment. Not one team member can possibly be expected to carry the ministry of the church. When the pastoral team is joined together by the appropriate discovery and identification of their spiritual gifts, then God provides the supply. *"From him the whole body, joined and held together by every supporting ligament, grows and builds itself up in love, as each part does its work" (Ephesians 4:16).*

An example from my team may prove helpful. There are outstanding qualities in my pastoral team that I admire, and frankly, don't possess. Let me cite a few examples. I love Jennifer's passion for the souls of children. I admire Eddie's pastoral heart for he embodies Christ's care for CCC. I am continually intrigued by and appreciative of Jim's ability to connect with total strangers. This long-legged Texan actually ate off a stranger's plate at a cool dive in Seattle. The stranger thought it was hilarious. I wanted to crawl under the table. Cecilia's heart of intercession for others is second to none. Kathryn's ability to do new things for the Lord during her "re-firement" years grants to me a model for my future. John's submission humbles me and enables me to be continually teachable as he so aptly demonstrates. Daren's cultural connection, creativity and life story make me appreciate God's sense of humor and His powerful sovereignty. Allison helps me remember that God is our ultimate cheerleader. Michele's gift of keeping the ministry moving forward in practical and concrete ways has saved me a free trip to the big building with a padded cell. Grayson's sensitivity to Christ in him is a continual reminder of my main source of power. Chris' sincerity as he leads various groups in worship throughout the week provides a freshness in my walk as I consider the powerful reality that God desires to meet with me because of his love for me.

This pastoral team embraces the vision that God gave to me for CCC. Further, we are locked arm in arm in pursuing the mission of winning souls and multiplying cells. Finally, we are passionate about seeing changed lives. I am a different man because of the influence that this team has made in my life. They are my friends and co-laborers. My greatest longing for any pastor or ministering Christian reading this book would be such a team.

Chapter Six

"Belonging and Believing"
(Need Oriented Evangelism)

YOU GOTTA DANCE...

The *Janger* was introduced in 1925 and became the first social dance in Bali where at least ten boys and ten girls dance and sing together. At the beginning of the dance, the participants sing a song that states who they are or where they come from (a name of a village). Expressed in this dance is the joy and satisfaction of being together and belonging to each other. During the dance, love, good times, and pleasant memories are expressed through song. The dance concludes with a corporate song of thanks and farewell.

The *Janger* is a dance of belonging and the participants believe that being together is preferred given the alternative of aloneness. Like a team who just won a coveted championship, they come together to celebrate—relishing a sense of community, call, and hope for the future.

DANCE WITH ME, DADDY

Machol [Hebrew]: A round dance with many participants, a chorus filled with celebration.

*"You turned my wailing into **dancing**; you removed my
sackcloth and clothed me with joy, that my heart may sing to
you and not be silent. O Lord my God, **I will give you
thanks forever"** (Psalm 30:11-12).*

*"Let them praise his name with **dancing** and **make
music to him** with tambourine and harp. For the Lord takes
delight in his people; he crowns the humble with salvation"
(Psalm 149:3-4).*

INTRODUCTION
**(by Jim Donaldson, Inter-generational Network Pastor,
CCC)**

One needs to look no further than the gospels to see that
meeting real needs is a powerful first step in leading people
to Christ. Jesus Christ, God in the flesh, spent His days
meeting the needs of people. We, too, live in a sea of need
and it is easy to be overwhelmed when we consider the
importance of meeting needs as a part of the Great
Commission. The words "go and make disciples" literally
mean "as you go, make disciples." As we go about our lives,
God is faithful to place people in our spheres of influence
who need to experience His grace through us. We can't
personally touch the whole world, but we can touch those
God places in our path. And for those we touch there is a
wide range of needs that He will give us the grace to meet.
The following is such an example that changed the course of
life for an entire family. The look on her face spoke volumes
about the burdens she carried as she waited tables at a local
restaurant. It was amazing how her face would light up as

we showed her kindness and treated her with dignity and respect. As we frequented the restaurant we tried to make sure they seated us in her section. The moment she saw us she would begin to smile as she greeted us. We began to pray that God would open a door for us to introduce her to Jesus. Over time she began to ask questions and we invited her to a cell meeting and to Sunday morning Celebration. "Next time I am off on Sunday I will come," she replied. After coming to a cell group for a few weeks she gave her life to Christ at Easter Sunday Celebration. Her countenance changed as she found purpose and companionship in her new life. Immediately, we began to pray for her husband. The Sunday she was baptized in the creek, he stood by the shore with tears in his eyes. We knew that it was just a matter of time before he surrendered to Christ. This couple had never experienced the love of Jesus in such a tangible way. They knew it was real because they were surrounded by a group of people that demonstrated His love consistently. The cell supported them emotionally as well as physically through acts of service and financial help.

Within a year, her husband became a Christian. They were eager to show this love to their not yet believing friends and immediately began to bring them to cell meetings. After a year had passed, they launched a new cell to reach more of their friends. Today they are part of the leadership team for a new church plant. Their lives are changed and their family has changed. It all began when others would simply welcome them into their midst. People treated them with dignity and respect. Evangelism begins with seeing people as being created in the image of God and deeply loved by Him. Reaching out to meet the needs of others seems natural as you live a lifestyle of love. A simple gesture in meeting a need can change the destiny of a family forever.

Ryan first met Jeff at the university's sound recording studio. A friendship developed and eventually Jeff was invited by Ryan to come to CCC's Celebration on Sunday morning. Jeff came with his wife, Doris. They were curious about the passion that so many expressed to Christ during Celebration. The message presented at Celebration filled Jeff with hope and a lot of questions. A strong tug of war ensued as Jeff began to contemplate his relationship with Christ. Yet, week after week, he would return, safely seated in a chair near the rear exit.

On a certain Sunday morning, Jeff was perplexed by a proclamation I communicated during a teaching. In the midst of making a point or two, I read *John 14:6: "Jesus answered, 'I am the way and the truth and the life. No one comes to the Father except through me.'"* Jeff thought, "Is Jesus the only way? What kind of arrogant statement is this guy making? What about other good people who pursue God in different ways besides selling their souls to Christ?" Jeff appropriately shared his concerns with Pastor Eddie who had met with him a few times over lunch. Eddie listened and offered no "quick fix" answers, gently allowing Jeff to wrestle openly and honestly with God. As the weeks unfolded, Jeff realized that Jesus was the way, and gave his life for him. He received Christ as Lord and Savior.

As the months progressed, a great celebration erupted as Pastor Eddie baptized his new friend, Jeff. Today, Jeff is shepherding a cell at CCC.

Troy is a wonderful and meticulous craftsman. He can turn old, cedar posts into beautiful works of art. To many, Troy emulates the Old West man with his lanky body, bushy mustache, tired blue jeans, pick up truck, sandy brown locks that flow down to his shoulders, and "Lonesome Dove" cowboy hat that covers his head. A college student, John, worked in a wood shop with Troy for a few weeks one hot, Texas summer. The two men became friends. Troy became intrigued with John's Jesus which eventually led him to a Celebration service at CCC.

On this certain Sunday morning, I noticed Troy immediately in the midst of the crowd. He soared over the other Celebration participants like an aspen tree situated among young oaks. As he took his seat, he removed his big cowboy hat and began to take in the time of praise and worship. I was intrigued with this cowboy and I introduced myself to him. God's Spirit was leading me to get to know Troy in a deeper way. Each week on a certain day, I would drive to a nearby town and meet with Troy over lunch. We became friends.

As the weeks progressed, Troy received Christ during a Celebration service at CCC. I was eager to see Troy following this life changing experience and asked him about his decision to receive Christ. Upon meeting him a few days later, I learned that he had opened up his rugged exterior to God and came to the realization that inside he was empty and needed Christ's friendship. It was a deep pleasure to not only baptize Troy in Cypress Creek, but to unite in marriage this powerful man and his love, Mary. The wedding ceremony was held in the front yard of their ranch house under an exquisite wood arch that Troy had crafted with his own hands. A few believers and a ton of not-yet believers gathered for the wedding celebration. One could sense God's thick presence amidst the dusty, wind blown yard of their stylish abode.

Andrew was a disciple of Jesus Christ. The scriptures teach us that Andrew was the first of Jesus' twelve disciples. Notice *John 1:40-42: "Andrew, Simon Peter's brother, was one of the two who heard what John [the Baptist] had said and who had followed Jesus. The first thing Andrew did was to find his brother Simon [Peter] and tell him, 'We have found the Messiah (that is, Jesus Christ).' And he brought him to Jesus."* In scripture, Andrew is known as the **"inviter"** who brought his own brother to meet Jesus. Further, he is the disciple who brought the boy with the loaves and fishes to Jesus. Think of the ramifications of his invitations. Think of his brother's enormous experience with Christ and his impact throughout the New Testament and even today. Think of Andrew's simple recruitment of a young boy to offer all that he had so that Christ might perform a miracle in the midst of thousands gathered to experience the living Messiah.

My friends Ryan and John are much like Andrew. Because of their passion for Christ, God has given to these men a deep passion to see God change lives. This is their heartbeat: Allowing others to experience a change of life through the touch of Jesus Christ. Ryan,

John and Andrew are synergists, connectors. They are not flaming evangelists prowling around condemning the "lost" to hell. They look like Jesus who was a "friend of sinners." These men were not and are not independent flyers, soaring through the lands seeing who they might target and "pick off" all in the name of Jesus. They are a part of a team—the body of Christ—the church today.

There is another exceptional quality that bears mentioning concerning Ryan, John and Andrew. They love their fellow man. They live out Christ's second greatest commandment of loving one another. For too long, the church has been playing the game of evangelism brimming full of gimmicks, guilt, condemnation and careless methodology. We do not have an evangelism training problem; we have a love problem.

I have a deep appreciation for mature adults (some would call these folks, "senior adults"). I love to listen to their stories of old and inquire what life was like in previous decades. I especially enjoy a good portion of this tribe who are grandparents. I'll tell you one thing that you already know. Grandparents love to talk about their grandchildren. I have seen numerous pictures of grandchildren proudly displayed by very proud grandparents. Yet, to this day, I have never had one grandchild seated next to me on an airplane say, "Excuse me, Sir. Would you like to see a picture of my grandparents?" I do not know one grandparent who attended any workshop that equipped him/her in how to talk to others about their grandchildren. You either get it or you don't! Grandparents talk about their grandchildren because they LOVE their grandchildren.

The root of sharing Christ with others is love for others. Simply put, the church needs to be reminded of God's love for the human soul. Pastor Philip Murdoch recently penned these words in a simple report about God's movement in his ministry region of South America.

What the members of the Costa Rican and Colombian churches have is Jesus' heart for the lost. I have not seen this so wide spread in any other church. Every member in the church understood and felt the weight and the value of a soul. In our churches, we invest a tremendous amount of time, money and effort managing our finances. But, how many dollars is a soul worth? We have been mediocre with the provision of souls the Lord has given us. We can't be mediocre with these souls the Lord has given us any longer.

Philip's passion for the human soul excites me and reminds me of God's deep love for every human being.

Paul prays for the church of Ephesus in the following manner. *"I pray that you will grasp how WIDE and LONG and HIGH and DEEP is the love of Christ"* (Ephesians 3:17-18). Assuredly, God's love is wide enough to include everybody (*Psalm 145:17, John 3:16*). This reality is the anchor of our security and self-esteem. Those who choose to tear down another individual have never fully realized the love of God. Further, God's love is long enough to last forever. *"(God says) I have loved you with an everlasting love...God's love will last for all time"* (Jeremiah 31:3, Psalm 69:2 GN).

Next, God's love is high enough to be everywhere. Let's admit it—human love wears out. This is why marriages bust up and families are shattered. Yet, God will never love you any more (or any less!) than He does right now. *"Neither height nor depth, nor anything else in all creation will be able to separate us from the love of God that is in Christ Jesus our Lord"* (Romans 8:39).

Finally, God's love is deep enough to meet your needs. Maybe you feel like the psalmist: *"My only hope is your love...for my problems are too big for me to solve and are piled over my head"* (Psalm 40:11 LB). The scripture grants us great comfort for *"we know and rely on the love God has for us...God is love"* (I John 4:16).

God is an intimate lover of the human soul. He created you to love you. He loves the person you love to hate. He loves the person who you believe is beyond His touch. He loves the person in the most desperate situation imaginable. His love is wide, long, high and deep. His love permeates and penetrates every nook and cranny of the world.

Years ago, two young Jewish women named Corrie Ten Boom and Betsy Ten Boom, were hiding from the evil Nazis in their home in the Netherlands. Eventually, they were discovered by the Nazis and assigned to a concentration camp. In great despair, Corrie said to Betsy, "This place is the pit of hell." Betsy quickly replied, "There is no pit so deep that God's love is not deeper."

Think of how Jesus had an all consuming and passionate love for the human soul. In Jesus' final days on earth, he prays in this manner to his father, *"My prayer is not for them [His disciples] alone. I pray also for those who will believe in me through their message" (John 17:20).* He prays for you and everyone that he created to receive his love. It was in the garden of Gethsemane that he made up his mind about you and me. It was not the soldiers who took Jesus out of the garden, but rather his decision to choose you and me. When he had to choose between spending eternity without you in heaven and going to hell for you, he chose hell. He would rather go to hell for you than go to heaven without you. While hanging on the cross, Christ could have walked away from you, but he didn't. He was and is the perfect model of his father's love for all mankind.

Let me introduce you to a man who you might find it difficult, if not impossible, to love. My friend, Pastor Kim (Pusan, Korea) tells a story of this man and how God's love was awakened in his church through the following experience. A Christian woman was married to an alcoholic man who frequently abused her. She was desperate for help, hope and support. The ladies of Pastor Kim's church formed a relationship with her and invited her to a ladies cell gathering. She was immediately accepted, fully loved and encouraged. As the weeks unfolded, trust was developed and this troubled woman began to share about her husband who worked in a local factory. She desperately wanted counsel about how to deal with her ungodly husband. She was encouraged by her fellow cell members to display the love and lifestyle of Christ to her husband. She heeded the advise of her cell members and waited for God to intervene in her desperate situation.

Eventually, her husband asked her, "What is it with you? I treat you like dirt, but you still love me, wash my clothes, make my meals, and care for our children." The woman responded, "I have changed because I have found others who believe in me and love me." Her husband probed deeper asking, "Who are these people?" She gently responded, "They are the church." To her surprise, her husband insisted on meeting these "church people." "Your love for me is so strong and continual, I've just got to see what you have found."

This alcoholic, abusive husband and father attended Celebration one Sunday morning with his wife. At the end of the service, he was Jell-O! His heart had been touched by God's Spirit, his sin had been revealed to him, and he desperately wanted to "make things right" with God. He received Christ as Lord. He has never touched another drop of alcohol, is a husband who loves his wife and children, and now leads a cell group (with his wife) in the church. Do you see the ministry of Andrew in the ladies of this church's cell group? Let me say again, no one is beyond the touch of God's love. God loves the human soul.

How important is "one" to you? Apparently, a multiplicity of businesses scattered throughout the globe understand the power of "one." For example, *The Guerilla Marketing Newsletter* reports that American Airlines calculated that if they had one more customer on each flight in a given year, the difference in revenue would have been about $114 million.[53] How much is one soul who is desperately loved by Jesus worth to God? How much is one soul worth to your church? There exists in the church today a love problem. How can this problem be solved? I believe through the eyes, ears and mouth. Let's look around us.

What do you notice about the people that live in your neighborhood? or stroll through the mall? or work in the next cubicle at your place of employment? What piques your interest in the works of art that fill our galleries, museums and stores? What do you hear from this culture? What are people talking about in your town's café? What is this generation's music saying to you? How about the movies, plays, dramas?

Matthew 11 grants to us an analogy of the church's current state of affairs. In this passage, Jesus is preaching in the towns of Galilee. When John the Baptist, who at this time is in prison, heard about what Christ was doing, he dispatched his disciples to ask Christ what he was up to. Further, he wanted to ask Jesus if *"he was the one who was to come, or should we expect someone else?" (Verse 3)*. Jesus replies to John's disciples by saying, *"Go back and report to John what you **hear** and **see**..." (Verse 4)*. The church must break out of her self-afflicted walls and locked up fortress to look into the heart of this culture. We must peer deeply, consistently into the soul of our homeland. Additionally, we must attune our eyes, ears and mouth to the beating heart of God through intercession.

Earlier in this chapter, I mentioned the power of the body of Christ working together as a team to share the love of Christ. For too long, we have owned an independent mind set, playing the evangelism game that suggests, "It's all up to me to win my friends to Christ." I, too, have participated in this man-centered game. (My goodness, I was trained to be a "Lone Ranger" in the context of evangelism.) John Finney, in his excellent book, *Recovering the Past: Celtic and Roman Mission*, alludes to this game as the old "Roman Model" of sharing Christ. This model entails Presentation (tell them the Christian message), Decision (Ask: "Are you ready to believe in Christ and become a Christian?"), and Fellowship ("Follow me to church.").[54] This is the model I followed. I don't regret my participation in this method of evangelism, but I certainly didn't experience immense support from other believers and consistently found myself debating the goodness of God with many skeptical individuals. Some individuals received Christ, but others were offended by my simple formula and predictable presentation.

It is my observation that most churches still do evangelism (if they attempt it at all) the "Roman" way. They may even employ an evangelism "professional" who is given the inevitable task of stirring up believers to reach others in confrontational evangelism techniques. Let's face the facts. We, as believers, know we are supposed to share Christ with others. We know that our not-yet believing friend's soul rests in the balance between heaven and hell. We are especially delighted that someone took the time to share the love of Christ with us. Yet, we don't evangelize. We are mesmerized by the "how to's," "when to do it," "who to do it to," and more.

I applaud George C. Hunter's work laid out in his book, *The Celtic Way of Evangelism*. Essentially, this book explains St. Patrick's methods of integrating his life into the Celtic culture (the "barbarians") during the 5th century. The sub-title to this book is "How Christianity Can Reach the West...Again." I believe Hunter grants some insightful tips as he builds on Finney's previous works.

Hunter writes:

> In significant contrast to contemporary Christianity's
> well known evangelism approaches of "Lone Ranger"
> one to one evangelism, or confrontational evangelism, or
> the public preaching crusade, (and in stark contrast to
> contemporary Christianity's more dominant approach of
> not reaching out at all!), we have [already] seen how the
> Celtic Christians usually evangelized as a team—by relat-
> ing to the people of a settlement; identifying with the
> people; engaging in friendship, conversation, ministry,
> and witness—with the goal of raising up a church in
> measurable time.[55]

Notice the vast difference from the "Roman" model expressed
in this evangelism methodology. The first goal of the Celtic
Christians was to establish a "common-union" with others. This
meant bringing the "barbarians" or pagans into the community of
faith. Next, in the context of this cell group or church fellowship,
conversations would evolve. These conversations were dialogical in
nature. The not-yet believing individual witnessed how believers
would pray and worship and see for himself the love of the
Christian community and the vivacious, life giving flow of ministry
to and with one another. He or she would experience "God showing
up" through actual miracles. As Hunter states, "in time, as they
[not-yet believers] discover what they now believe, you invite them
to commit."[56]

Now, don't miss this Celtic model's progression of evangelism.
Fellowship occurs followed by ministry and conversations. In due
time, an individual was invited to commit his/her life to Christ.
Look again at Hunter's quote above. Do you see the words, "in
time." I love these words. Maybe you have erred as I have distinguishing between "God's time" and "your time." Winning a soul to
Christ is all about God's timing in a person's life. We have the privilege of participating in this event, but only through God's power
and love in and through us. Can we trust God's timing in the lives of
our friends?

Recently, I had the privilege of uniting in marriage Roy and Ruby. Roy was employed by a gentleman in our church who is a fine disciple of Christ. This disciple emulated the model of Andrew and invited Roy to come and see Christ at CCC. Roy turned up one Sunday morning with his girlfriend (at the time), Ruby. Roy and Ruby sensed that they were disconnected from God and needed Christ as their foundation. As the months progressed, Ruby received Christ and was baptized in an old horse trough right in front of CCC's Worship Center. This was a great time of celebration. As Roy and Ruby's relationship grew, the "M" word was openly discussed and they decided to talk with me about getting married. I spoke with Roy and Ruby's cell group leaders and members and decided that I wanted to know these two individuals in a deeper way. Therefore, I met with them for pre-marital counseling.

During the first session, I clearly articulated the gospel of Christ and simply asked, "Have y'all experienced receiving Christ into your life?" Ruby immediately responded, "Oh, yes. I asked my cell network pastor to tell me how I could receive Christ at the women's Encounter weekend. Right there, I received Christ." With tears streaming down her face, she conversed with me of her assurance that Christ loved her completely and died so that she might have new life. At this point in our gathering, I turned to Roy without saying a word.

He took my non-verbal cue and stated, "Look, my boss got me here to CCC and you have kept me here." This comment piqued my interest and I asked, "How have I kept you here?" He responded with a word of encouragement to me which I treasure to this day. He continued, "I love everything I see and hear. This place is awesome, but I got to tell you something, Pastor Rob. I haven't crossed over yet." I smiled at Roy and said, "Great, man! I love working with honest seekers. Let's carry on with the task at hand." We resumed our conversation on Christian marriage.

A few more sessions transpired over the weeks and the day of the big wedding was upon Roy and Ruby. The wedding party gathered in their appropriate places and exactly five minutes before the wedding ceremony began, I summoned Roy to a side room. "Roy," I looked deep into his eyes, "Have you crossed over yet?" He connected immediately with my question based on our prior discussion. In my heart and mind, I was looking forward to sharing with the folks present at the wedding celebration that Roy had just received Christ as his Lord. With a slight hint of nervousness in his voice, he stated, "Pastor Rob, I'm still crossing over, but I'm not there yet." At this precise moment, God gripped my heart. I sensed his quiet whisper, "Rob, what will it be, my time or your time?" I responded to God without uttering a word, "Your time, God. Always your time."

Roy and Ruby were married. They are in a cell group together and present in Celebration. Roy is still an honest seeker of Christ and I know that God's Spirit is continually wooing his heart to receive Christ. My friend, I have an open and honest confession that I want to share. I believe I could have had my way that wedding day with Roy. I could have pressed him into a relationship with Christ. But, I didn't. It was "my time!" The words of John Wesley reverberated in my mind, "If you cannot reason or persuade a man into the truth, never attempt to force him into it. If love will not compel him to come in, leave him to God, the Judge of all." I know in my "knower" that Roy and Ruby know the love of Christ through me and the many other believers at CCC. Further, I know that I am not alone in my desire to see Roy receive Christ. I am a member of a team—the body of Christ.

Let's revisit the Celtic model of evangelism. John Finney observes that the Celts believed in "the importance of the team. A group of people can pray and think together. They inspire and encourage each other. The single entrepreneur is too easily prey to self doubt and loss of vision."[57] I concur completely with Finney's observation and have experienced numerous times the power of believers working together to see others come to receive Christ. Let me share more about this possibility in your church through a few stories.

The cold wind blew through the eighty-three year old woman's hair as she was chauffeured through the village streets of Wimberley, Texas. She was bundled tight as layer after layer of clothing kept her warm fighting off the chilling elements of the day. It was her first time to ride in the side car of a Harley Davidson. Her driver was Sargent. He was indeed a "Hog lover" clad in black leather from head to toe. His skull cap covered the bald spot on the top of his head as his long black hair flew freely behind his body. The drivers of the passing vehicles smiled amusingly. Other spectators chuckled and shook their heads repeatedly in disbelief.

Grace had only known Sargent for a few weeks and he was taking her to Thanksgiving dinner at his home. His wife, Kitty, was busy at home preparing the turkey and fixings as her three children scurried under her feet in the modest kitchen. This eighty-three year old, grandmother was not fearful. She was on a mission. Allow me to digress for just a moment. We'll catch up with Grace, Sargent and Kitty in a few shakes.

It was September 14, 1996 when I attended the "Growing a Healthy Church" Conference led by Dann Spader of Sonlife Ministries. After thirteen years in the ministry, I must admit that many of the concepts that were shared in this conference were not new. My ulterior motive in attending the conference was simply to expose my fellow overseers (elders) to Biblical principles for growing a healthy church. Then, Dann threw me a curve ball. I had always believed it to be true, but I had difficulty articulating my persuasion concerning evangelism in the church. The curve ball was Dann's explanation of the "5.3 Principle" which states:

> A typical unchurched person must get to know at least 5.3 believers relationally before they will trust the message of Christianity. Research also shows that they must hear that message five to seven times before they fully understand it.[58]

This principle is what I had been searching for in my quest to motivate others to participate in sharing the life changing message of Jesus Christ.

In my estimation, the church has been failing in true conversion growth for decades. Aubrey Malphurs refers to this phenomenon as the "shrinking American church."[59] Dr. Win Arn reports that 80 to 85 percent of the churches in America have either "plateaued" or are dying. While the typical church in America is declining, the unchurched population is growing. Dr. George Gallup conducted a survey in 1978 and discovered that 41 percent of America was unchurched. He conducted the same survey in 1988 and the figure had climbed to 44 percent.[60] These statistics and indicators of today's church rattled through my mind as I pondered the 5.3 Principle. Then, I began to think about deer season.

Yes, deer season. I am an avid hunter. I join thousands of hunters each year in this ritual and ensuing pursuit of the "big buck." I even dream at night about "bagging" a monster buck that has eluded other hunters for years. I relish the sight of a big buck strapped on top of a sport utility vehicle jetting down a country road. The majority of weekend warriors return home with no trophies, only spell-binding stories about what almost happened.

It has been my observation that evangelism in the church today is akin to spiritual deer hunting season. Church folks are motivated solely by the end result— the big prize of salvation for another's soul. This motivation carries them through dense foliage enveloped in freezing temperatures shouldering alone the burden of the hunt. Hunting is not a team sport. It is about what "I" saw, what "I" pursued, what "I" slew with my .270 Remington.

Reginald Bibby accurately describes the American church with these words:

> When evangelicals talk about their successes in evangelism they are frequently inaccurate at best and dishonest at worst. For too long, many evangelicals have equated church growth with outreach, failing to differentiate between their net numerical gains and their success in reaching non-professing Christians.... Seven out of every 10 new members come from other evangelical churches, while two in 10 are the children of evangelicals. Only about one in 10 new members come from outside of the evangelical community.[61]

After returning from the conference, I immediately sent out a letter to seventeen individuals explaining the 5.3 Principle, asking for their participation in testing this principle. The enthusiastic respondents (ten) were gathered together at a leadership retreat and

I taught a seminar based on this principle. It was my conviction that each respondent received a thorough understanding of how he/she might be used of God to reach their not-yet believing friends.

The participants in this project were first asked to target one or two people in their `oikos' or sphere of influence. This challenge gave the participants a point of focus to intentionally share the life of Jesus Christ. Oikos is the New Testament word for household (*Luke 10:1-7; Acts 20:20*) which comes from the word `oikonomos' which means a steward. An oikos is defined as a social system composed of common human groupings including kinship, community and interest.

An oikos refers to relationships established through people with common interests, goals, problems, age and more.[62] David Finnell explains that "the most obvious and important oikos in life is one's personal oikos.... the people in your daily life that you spend thirty to forty-five minutes with each week."[63] These are the people with whom one has a right to relationship. "A right to relationship is a culturally defined right to interact and communicate with another person who has a culturally defined obligation or desire too respond."[64]

The idea is Biblical and simple. Once someone has received Christ, then that individual can reach her own oikos for Christ in a way that the multitudes cannot do alone.

Next, the participants and the names of the not-yet believers were released to the Prayer Ministry teams. Naturally, each participant was challenged and encouraged to pray daily for their not-yet believing friends. Ed Silvoso writes, "Prayer is the most tangible trace of eternity in the human heart. Intercessory prayer on behalf of the felt needs of the lost is the best way to open their eyes to the light of the gospel."[65] The apostle Paul instructed Timothy and the church to participate in praying for all men. He wrote, *"First of all, then, I urge that entreaties and prayers, petitions and thanksgivings, be made on behalf of all men, for kings and all who are in authority, in order that we may lead a tranquil and quiet life in all godliness and dignity" (1 Timothy 2:1).* The key words in this passage as it relates to praying for those in one's oikos are *'all men.'* The participants in the process were continually encouraged to bathe their not-yet believing friends in prayer.

Colossians 4:2-6 reiterates this necessary element as one seeks to reach the not-yet believer. This passage teaches that evangelism, spiritual warfare, and prayer are so intertwined that it is hard to separate them. Our witness depends on prayer, the Holy Spirit and becoming an available vessel for the Lord to use. Jesus modeled prayerful dependence upon the Father during His earthly ministry. In the gospels (a period of forty months), Jesus quietly slipped away to pray on at least forty-seven occasions.[66] Carl Wilson adds:

> Prayer is one of the most important aspects of building disciples. If one is to help others grow in the knowledge of Jesus Christ, he must pray. Indeed, if one does everything else in terms of building disciples, yet fails to pray, nothing significant will happen.[67]

On a recent visit to a number of churches in Korea, I strolled past a sign posted by a main thoroughfare running through the streets of Seoul that captivated my attention. The sign was a simple bus schedule that informed the believers at Yoido Full Gospel Fellowship when the free bus would be departing for Prayer Mountain. My friend and host, Paul Jeong, explained to me that every hour on the hour, every day of the year, a bus departed from the main church campus to this place of prayer. I remember gazing at the sign for a few minutes, then fumbling through my backpack for my digital camera in order to share this captivating "bus stop sign" with my friends back home. Immediately, I spun around and noticed the four to five buses (big buses, with large, loud diesel engines!) that were jam packed with intercessors departing for this place of prayer which is a one hour drive away. These photos from my camera are absolutely meaningless without the explanation that you have been privy to. This church's Prayer Mountain is not the only place of prayer in this country. Numerous churches have purchased "high places" throughout the country to intercede for their not-yet believing friends, family members, colleagues, neighbors and peers. No wonder Korea is home to some of the largest evangelistic churches in the world. Intercession is the key that unlocks hardened hearts in our spheres of influence.

The third phase of the process involves the believers intentionally introducing their not-yet believer friends to other believers. Furthermore, each participant was encouraged to be deliberate in exposing his not-yet believing friends to hearing the message of Christ at least five to seven times through various avenues. This aspect of the process was accomplished in a multitude of ways which I will later discuss.

As the facilitator of this process, I must comment on three essentials necessary for healthy participation in testing the 5.3 Principle. First, the facilitator must frequently check in with the participants. This requires availability. I contacted each participant by phone, letter or note every seven to ten days. I never "pushed" the process on them and always strayed away from "judging" their progress. I listened intently and provided necessary resources and encouragement. (A grave mistake could be made by a process facilitator who does not check in regularly with the process participants).

Second, it is imperative to recruit participants who have a heart for seeing their friends receive Christ. This also requires availability. I learned that the "well-educated" believer who chose to participate was not necessarily intentional in reaching his or her oikos for Christ. I was greatly pleased and amazed at many of the participants who had little equipping in evangelism. They oozed with excitement each step in the process. They experienced God arranging the circumstances of their day and receiving answers from him in prayer. They were on a mission! Simply put, look to the heart over the head.

Third, a process facilitator must consistently remind the participants that the believer is a mouthpiece and vessel in the hands of a sovereign God. I repeatedly said to the participants, "We don't save anyone...This is God's work...Pray and make the most of every opportunity." When these words would land on a participant's ears and heart, I could sense immediate peace and release of trying to conjure up something from the minds of men, but not from the heart of God.

One of my participants was Kathryn. Kathryn received Christ in her forties. Evangelism was not a priority in her church life and only in recent years has she received equipping in personal evangelism. She is retired, but extremely active in various facets of the community including social clubs and the ministry of the church. She is a network cell pastor and has had tremendous success in multiplying new cells in the past several years. She is articulate, delightful, submissive and an influencer in the church.

In the summer of 1994, the Lord began to work on an underdeveloped area of her spiritual life. I was overseeing some personal witnessing encounters near a beautiful lake outside of Monterrey, Mexico. Many believers in the group were sharing Christ with the local children, young people and adults. Kathryn sternly grabbed me by my arm. She stated, "I need your help. Follow me." She led me to a young man on a horse and encouraged me to share Christ with him. Kathryn stood close by mentally taking notes of the encounter. When the young man galloped off on his horse, she began to explain how she had never been in a one-on-one witnessing encounter before. It was new to her, but she was not fearful.

Two years later, Kathryn noticed Jackie in the beauty salon. Kathryn began to make small talk and the conversation turned to the church. Jackie stated to Kathryn, "I've noticed the people in town who go to your church." Kathryn asked, "What do you notice about them?" Jackie responded, "They all seem to glow!" This was the beginning of Kathryn's deliberate attempt to share Christ with Jackie and her husband, Joe.

Because of Kathryn's teachable spirit, she quickly committed to testing the 5.3 Principle. Kathryn has had immense success utilizing evangelistic dinners through the life of her cell group. She determined to use the same approach with Jackie and Joe with one minor adjustment. Instead of her whole cell coming over for dinner, Kathryn determined to invite only one believing couple (Ted and Becky) to enjoy dinner with Jackie and Joe. Kathryn knew that Ted had known Jackie and Joe for years. Joe had great respect for Ted and they spoke frequently when seeing each other in town.

The dinner event finally arrived and Kathryn was well prepared to facilitate the discussion around the table. A delightful conversation filled the room. There was great laughter and reminiscing over the years and past events. Kathryn gently began to share about her relationship with Christ. Ted shared how he had received Christ years ago and exclaimed, "I can't imagine what kind of condition I would be in if it weren't for Jesus." Jackie and Joe were receptive and the various couples disbanded for the evening.

Kathryn continued to intertangle her life and lives of other believers with Jackie and Joe. She was meticulous in inviting Jackie and Joe to Celebration and cell gatherings on at least three occasions. Jackie and Joe consider Kathryn to be a trusted friend. They relish the time that they spend with her. Kathryn has shared with Jackie and Joe how they might receive Christ. The journey continues!

As the facilitator of this project, I learned that I needed to be available, encourage and emphasize the participants to allow Christ to work through them. I also learned that I must model. To me, this meant being an active participant in the process of testing the 5.3 Principle. This bred a spirit of "teamness" among the participants. We frequently shared our successes, failures, strategies and suggestions. Our hearts were knit closer together in community through the power of prayer and deeper fellowship.

Here's my story. It was an exceptionally busy day at the church office. I had seriously thought about packing it up and heading for the house just to have some quiet study time. I shuffled through the messages on my desk finding a message to please call 'Kitty.' I did not know a 'Kitty.' With the number of calls that I am asked to return, this conspicuous message from Kitty was probably going to end up in the round file. But, not today! I made the call only to get a strange message on an answering machine. I left my name and number and hurried on to my next call.

Two weeks passed and I had completely forgotten about that call to Kitty. My administrative assistant paged me and informed me that a desperate sounding lady was on 'Line 1.' I trusted my assistant and decided to take the call. It was Kitty. She could not fully articulate her distress at the moment, but insisted on seeing me accompanied by her live in boyfriend, Sargent. I agreed and we scheduled an appointment.

The next day, they walked into my office. It was easy for me to determine that they were "bikers." Even though they were in a pastor's office, they did not shy away from their everyday, common street language. They were both brutally honest...and I liked them. Kitty explained her years of pursuing God only to be judged by church folks. She finally gave up on the church and desperately tried to find her own way. I asked her, "Why are you here today...talking with me...a pastor?" She replied, "I called every church in town and you were the only pastor to return my phone calls." Humbled that I wasn't her sole "pick of the litter," we began to talk about the things of God. No... "they" talked about God...I listened.

At the end of our initial visit, I explained how God was wooing them to his heart throughout the years. I told them that I was willing to work with them based on three conditions. First, they would need to meet other people in the community ("believers") by being present each week in a cell. Second, they would need to complete each action step that I would give them as the counselor. Finally, they would need to bring their family to Celebration each Sunday. Kitty expressed how she was willing to go to a cell meeting and complete each action point. She, however, was totally unwilling to go to "big church" because the environment frightened her tremendously. I agreed to the amended agreement and we began to brainstorm what type of cell environment would be most conducive for their family. I assured them that they would receive a phone call from a shepherd to invite them to their cell meeting.

As I pondered Kitty and Sargent's lot in life throughout the week, I was reminded of the 5.3 Principle. A gentle voice was reminding me, "Rob, you need not do this alone." I picked up the phone and called a cell shepherd and described my recent meeting with Kitty and Sargent. To my delight, the shepherd was highly enthusiastic about meeting Kitty and Sargent. To date, this couple knows at least fifty believers. Frequently during our sessions together, they have expressed to me that the greatest time of their week is sitting in the midst of the people in their cell. They especially appreciate one dear prayer warrior in their group whose name is Grace.

Recently, Grace called me and asked me a curious question. "Pastor Rob," she stated, "do you think it would be okay for me to go to Kitty and Sargent's house for Thanksgiving dinner?" I was elated, but I wanted Grace to make the decision on where she would spend Thanksgiving. I asked, "Do you want to go to their house?" She answered, "Absolutely...yes." I encouraged her to go. She hesitated and began slowly to tell me more. "Pastor Rob, there is one thing I think you should know. Sargent wants to pick me up on his motorcycle for Thanksgiving dinner. What should I do about that?" Not really knowing how to respond, I pursued a typical pastoral route and asked her, "Have you prayed about riding on Sargent's motorcycle?" She said that indeed she had prayed and God had told her, "Try it, Grace, you'll like it!" I roared with laughter.

At my last visit with Kitty and Sargent, they expressed the awesome power of prayer that was experienced in their cell meeting. Kitty explained, "We gathered around several of the group members and began to pray for them. I was weeping and Sargent was weeping. Our children were placing their hands on the adults in the group asking God to work in their lives. The group even prayed for us..." She could not finish her explanation because of her joyous tears. At that precise moment, I was prompted to explain clearly how one may receive Christ. The discussion lasted nearly forty minutes because the questions, comments and experiences that Kitty and Sargent offered. They both received and reconfirmed their commitment to Christ. The journey continues!

As one can see, the 5.3 Principle emphasizes "body life" evangelism. For too long in church life, a believer has believed the subtle message that he alone must win his friends to Christ. He is the "Lone Ranger" evangelist trying to be perfect in his lifestyle and gospel presentations. This has led to many believers feeling frustrated, ill-equipped and unworthy of being a mouthpiece for God. The participants in this project expressed great anticipation and relief knowing that they could simply serve as a "gospel synergist" for their not-yet believing friend. The participants acknowledged the power of the Christian community covenanting together to reach others for Christ. This sentiment was shared repeatedly as reflected by the following comments by the participants:

- "I have always felt that I was not alone in this process. My believing friends did not even know many times they were being used of God to help win my lost friend to Christ. I experienced a calmness in my spirit and confidence that God would arrange the circumstances in His perfect way and timing."

- "I knew that I was being covered by my Christian friends in prayer. I experienced unusual boldness and power as I related with my lost friend. I have time and time again forgot the awesome power of prayer in reaching people for Christ."

- "I've never seen myself as an evangelist. I still don't believe I am an evangelist...and that is fine! I know now that I can depend on my brothers and sisters in Christ to assist me in reaching a not-yet believer for Christ."

- "God allowed me to surround my not-yet believing friend with dozens of believers. They were caught before they even knew they were caught. They love Jesus now because they saw the life of Jesus through His body."

- "Frankly, I greatly feared the day that I would have to share Christ with my lost friend. This is new to me. The moment came so naturally...just as easy as breathing. The explanation of the gospel and my own personal testimony were out of my mouth before I knew what happened. I am relieved and can't wait until God uses me again to share Himself with `number two' on my oikos list."

These comments are verbal manifestations of a greater Biblical truth. *"The body is a unit, though it is made up of many parts; and though all its parts are many, they form one body....Now you are the body of Christ, and each one of you is a part of it"* *(I Corinthians 12:12,14)*. The church today would be strengthened in her evangelistic endeavors if we peered through this lens of body life. The believer need not take on full responsibility of being *all* parts of the body to *all* people. This is ill-Biblical, frustrating and lacks productivity. Finally, it was encouraging to see how the not-yet believer desired a taste of Christian community. Tim Celek and Dieter

Zander help one to understand this desire in the heart of a not-yet believer utilizing the words of Douglas Coupland:

> Now—here is my secret: I tell it to you with an openness of heart that I doubt I shall ever achieve again, so I pray that you are in a quiet room as you hear these words. My secret is that I need God— that I am sick and can no longer make it alone. I need God to help me give, because I no longer seem to be capable of giving; to help me be kind, as I no longer seem capable of kindness; to help me love, as I seem beyond being able to love.[68]

Writing concerning "Generation X," Celek and Zander propose, "Inclusiveness and community are values they cherish more than truth."[69] I believe that this proposition can be expanded to include the majority of one's not-yet believing friends who are looking for life and Christ through his body, the church.

Do you remember a previous chapter in this book entitled, "The Power of Story?" Please know the *power of story* can make a revolutionary difference in how you go about sharing *His-story*. In our quest to share his story, we can become mechanical, goal driven, and void of empathy. "One reason the gospel is not heard or people don't want to hear it is because the image of Christians is that they are not only self-righteous but arrogant people who know everything and have nothing to learn from anyone outside themselves."[70] Do those you desperately want to reach for Christ have a story? Sure. Do you have to agree with every facet of their life's philosophy contained in their story? No. But, "the conviction of Christians is that everybody's individual story is valuable because they are made in the image of God."[71] Displaying compassion for others by listening to others fosters relationship and community.

A certain father was desperately looking forward to an afternoon nap. His son, however, wanted his dad's attention. The father noticed a page of the newspaper lying on the floor featuring a map of the world. The father quickly tore the newspaper into pieces and instructed his son to put the "puzzle" back together. He promised his son that once this task was completed, then he would play with him. Ten minutes later, the son returned with the map of the world perfectly in place. The father responded by saying, "Why, that's incredible! How did you get that put together so fast?" His son replied, "It was easy dad. Can't you see? On the other side of the page was a picture of a person. Once I put my person together, the world looked just fine."[72]

This is the message of the 5.3 Principle: Believers striving through God's Spirit to piece together a broken and tattered world one person at a time.

Let's take a time out before I conclude this chapter with a review of the main points.

- Evangelism is a team sport that the whole body of Christ is called to play.

- If your church lacks an evangelistic fervor, then your church has a love problem.

- God loves the human soul. Let's be like God.

- Intercession is the key that unlocks the hardened hearts in our spheres of influence.

- The 5.3 Principle teaches us that "Lone Ranger" evangelism is not the most effective approach.

- Listen to the story of others as you long to share *His-story.*

Allow me to bring clear focus to this discussion on evangelism. The church today must re-learn (or learn for the first time) the reality that for most people, "belonging comes before believing."[73] The sundry of stories you read in this chapter underscore this truth. The key to allowing not-yet believers (even "barbarians") the opportunity to belong to your cell group or church fellowship is grace. Please be reminded that evangelism is a gift of grace given by the Holy Spirit to exalt Jesus Christ, and therefore, build up the body of Christ.

You can be a grace giver or a grace killer. You can choose the following alternatives to grace: works, a list of 'do's and 'don't,' or a dogmatic lifestyle laced with judgment. I challenge you to live a life of grace. *Romans 14* grants practical guidelines for grace givers. First, a grace giver accepts others (*vv. 1-4*). Next, a grace giver refuses to dictate to others which allows God the freedom to direct one's life (*vv. 5-8*). Third, a grace giver never assumes a position in another person's life that only God can fulfill *(vv. 9-12)*. Finally, a grace giver encourages peace and the unity of others (*v. 19*).

Let's go back to the epitome of God's grace, Jesus Christ. *"The Word became flesh and made his dwelling among us. We have seen his glory, the glory of the One and Only; who came from the Father, full of grace and truth" (John 1:14). "Be strong in the grace that is in Christ Jesus" (2 Timothy 2:1). "For it is by grace you have been saved, through faith—and this not from yourselves, it is the gift of God—not by works, so that no one can boast" (Ephesians 2:8-9).* Believing in grace is one thing; living it is another. Grace received but unexpressed is dead grace.

Surely you have heard that you "ought" to share Christ with not-yet believers. There are many other "oughts" that have weighed heavy on me during my Christian life. I call these many "oughts"— "oughteries." Evangelism is one of these "oughteries." I have learned in recent years the power of changing my "oughteries" into opportunities. Once you have had the opportunity of seeing and participating in the most incredible miracle this side of heaven— when the supernatural (God) touches the natural (man) invading that heart with the Holy Spirit, then you will never turn back. Ponder this Chinese poem in the context of evangelism, "belonging comes before believing," and changing your "oughteries" into opportunities to extend God's grace and salvation to others:

Go to the people.
Live among them.
Learn from them.
Love them.
Start with what they know.
Build on what they have.

Chapter Seven

"Whistles and Boilers"
(Functional Structures)

YOU GOTTA DANCE...

Ori Pahu is a competition dance between dancers and drummers. With frantic excitement, the dancers keep pace with the drumbeats as the drummers slow down or speed up the tempo. This dance requires hefty endurance for it may last as long as five minutes or more. Both dances and drummers are judged on various required hip and feet movement, presentations, and costumes.

Functional structures and life giving ministry need not be competing elements. In the *Ori Pahu*, both the drummers and the dancers are required. For God's dancing hand to be in your midst, consider the necessity of the beating drum and lively dancers.

DANCE WITH ME, DADDY

The **Dance of Procession** is an orderly and reverent dance that prepares individuals for a move of God.

"Walk about Zion, go around her, count her towers, consider well her ramparts, view her citadels, that you may tell of them to the next generation. For this God is our God for ever and ever; he will be our guide even to the end" *(Psalm 48:12-14).*

INTRODUCTION
(by Michele Gooch, CCC's Operations Manager and Network Pastor)

We recently constructed a building with the help of some well-known architects. In the design stage, the architects asked us about the function of the building. "What's going to happen there?" they quipped. They believed the form of the building needed to follow the function of the building. The same is true for church life. The form or structure is determined by the function. You must first ask yourself, "What are you trying to accomplish?" Is your goal to win and disciple souls? If so, then your structure cannot be about power, authority figures, a specific personality or possessiveness. Instead, it must be about teamwork. When you create a structure based on teams, you have viability which leads to multiplication and reproduction. Teamwork produces the appropriate environment for birth and growth. All living beings exist within a structure. Without the physical body a human being has no life. Therefore, structure and life are not opposites but complements to each other.

At CCC, each cell group is a team. The cell members come together to win souls in their neighborhood, their workplace, and their families. As a team, they support each other in life. Likewise, the leaders of several cell groups form a team purposing to equip the people in their cells in a powerful and effective manner. To work together as a team you have to share the same vision. A beautiful illustration of this is music. To create a vocal ensemble you can't just put a bunch of soloists together. The sound each member makes has to mesh with the sound the next person makes. It's not about showcasing one person's ability; it's about creating one, complete sound.

When you look at a sports team, you notice they not only practice together and play together, they also travel together and hang out together. Generally, they share life together. This is the way the teams at CCC work. Yes, we may come together to accomplish a specific task but our teams are more than that because we invest in each other's lives. These teams pull off incredible things week after week. Things like outrageous weekends designed to bring freedom to people; huge evangelistic events created to reach the lost world; a well planned equipping track shaped to move disciples into leaders; and powerful mission trips fashioned to support local pastors and churches. Most gifted, talented people guided by the Holy Spirit are already doing some of that.

Team structure allows you to handle tasks efficiently because teams already know the gifting of their individual team members. The unexpected is even easily dealt with because you don't have to pull together a committee. You already have a team in place. Teams keep the focus on the vision and a balance between order and change. They allow the whole system to be flexible and reproducible.

Abraham Lincoln once squelched a particularly offensive heckler by suddenly stopping his speech, turning directly toward the offender, and noting to the audience:

This noisy friend reminds me of a certain steamboat

that used to run on the Illinois River. It was an energetic boat, was always busy. When they built it, however, they made one serious mistake, this error being in the relative sizes of the boiler and the whistle. The latter was usually busy, too, and people were aware that it was in existence. This particular boiler to which I have referenced was a six-foot one and did all that was required of it in the way of pushing the boat along; but as the builders of the vessel had made the whistle a six-foot one, the consequence was that every time the whistle blew the boat had to stop.[74]

For clarity, I trust that you know that steam made in the boiler to move the boat is also the steam the whistle uses to blow. Today, an abundance of churches have overbearing whistles that retard the boiler of effective and efficient ministry. The policy and procedures are intact. The van usage policy (designed by a retired Air Force Master Sargent) comes complete with a glossary of terms for clarity and comprehension. The church's constitution is as tight as a drum. Using the church's parlor for a worthwhile gathering requires a majority vote at *next month's* regularly scheduled business meeting. An understandable reading of the bylaws requires a pre-law degree. The organizational chart looks like a maze, fitfully laid out on a sheet of paper the size of a place mat that protects the dining room table from messy gravy spills. Everything has a place and is in place. Yet, church life is as dry as sucking on a piece of white chalk. The whistle has overpowered the church's main purpose. The church chugs along with the laborious pace of a barge.

This type of structural paralysis and atrophy is not of God. Rather, it is about man's need to control, predict, anticipate and regulate the endless possibilities that "just may happen to us if we're not careful." Let me be straight with you. Church is messy...or it should be. You see, the church is about relationships. The primary relationship that the church should take interest in is her relationship to God. Is your relationship with God always neat, in order, precise, easy to document? Or is it messy, erratic, even confusing at times? You might consider how various men and women throughout the ages would classify their relationship with

God. Think of Moses, Abraham, Job, Peter, Rahab or Mary (the mother of Jesus).

The church is also about relationships with other believers. Do you really like every believer that you know? Are you excited when seated next to him/her at a dinner party? Are there not inevitable relational conflicts that you will face with your fellow believers? Further, the church has a relationship with the not-yet believing world. Do you have a good, poor or average friendship with the not-yet believing world? As you minister to a not-yet believer, are the church's bylaws, constitution, policies and procedures foremost in your mind? Yes, church life is messy; not wrapped in a neat little package which never comes unraveled.

Now, please don't misunderstand. I believe and encourage you to value structure. I love discussions about various church structures and think often of my own church's structure. I am in no way encouraging sloppiness, half-heartedness or unprofessional habits, activities and ministries. My encouragement is to have a very simple structure that appropriately reflects God's specific vision and mission for your church. Additionally, align your church's structure with the Great Commandment and Great Commission. These pursuits keep your boiler hot and allows you to disregard obnoxious whistles.

My friend, Mario Vega, pastors the Mission Cristiana Elim Church in San Salvador, El Salvador. This church's structure is simply awesome with a heavy dose of accountability and purposive ministry. I would venture to say that you would be highly impressed with Elim's structure or system. The structure is the backbone of Elim in this impoverished country. Elim is sleek, fast on their feet, responsive, and effective. Mario shares one example that underscores this reality.

On Saturday, January 13, 2001, I took my 10-year-old son shopping in San Salvador, El Salvador. The kind manager of the bookstore we visited opened the door for me, but immediately locked the door after I entered because there had been so many robberies in the area. Once inside, I greeted the manager and the person in charge of the stock room who then left to find the sales person for me.

I looked down at my watch and noticed it was 11:35 a.m. At that very moment the earthquake struck. It began very softly, almost imperceptible. In a country like El Salvador where earthquakes are quite frequent, a person develops a certain instinct to measure the intensity of a quake. I have developed this internal mechanism as well, and it is set off when the danger level passes a certain point. Although the earthquake was still very soft, I laid everything in my hands on a desk and immediately grabbed my son, who was unaware.

As the earthquake increased in strength, I looked for a solid structure under which we could find shelter, but I found none. The manager returned, completely paralyzed by what was happening. I instinctively said to him, "Open the door!" These words startled him back to his senses. He took his key, opened the door and we fled the bookstore as I tried to calm my son.

As I walked through the street I could see the power lines shaking like a leaf in the wind and the cables were bouncing up and down. I found a place that seemed safe, but then the earthquake began to grow in strength. Car alarms all around us were blaring and people were screaming as they ran into the streets. I looked up to see the house in front of me lose its roof and fall into the street as the house crumbled. As I turned to the right, I saw an apartment complex four stories high waving back and forth. Each shift produced loads of dust and I grieved for those who were on the fourth floor.[75]

Mario and his son survived the forty-five endless seconds of devastation. However, 1,262 people lost their lives, 5,565 were injured and 1,364,160 lost their homes. Seventeen people from Elim died and 1,409 families lost their homes, including six pastors. The Elim church's youth building suffered extensive damage and the main worship center was declared unsafe for the 35,000 worshipers expected the very next day for the six Celebration services. How would Mario and his pastors effectively communicate with the thousands concerning this dilemma? I'll let Mario tell you the story:

> Through the radio, I shared with our church the condition of our buildings and our plan to meet under each cell network throughout the city. I asked our leaders and pastors to organize services to communicate all the details through our [radio] station. The section supervisors began contacting their leaders and together they stayed in contact with their zone pastors. In a matter of minutes, the leaders communicated through the radio, telling their people what to do and where to meet. Some cells formed congregational meetings in the street, schools, city squares or camp settings.
>
> With the help of the radio, we were able to give information to the more than 106,000 people who attend our weekly cell groups. The people turned out in mass to each one of the respective services. The gospel was preached and hundreds of people gave their lives to Jesus Christ.[76]

Mario and his people didn't stop there. As the government was gathering information concerning the extent of the damage, the people of Elim church were amassing aid to needy families and ministering in the disaster-ridden areas of the city.

The earthquakes didn't stop there, either. Exactly one month after this first earthquake, a second earthquake rocked and split this country's land killing 407 people and leaving an additional 252,622 people homeless. The damage levied by these two earthquakes totaled $1.25 billion. The Elim church responded with immediacy and love for their hurting comrades. To date, this church has sent 208 tons of clothes, food and blankets to the affected families. Further, Mario is leading the Elim church to rebuild at least 500 homes.

But, there's more! According to Mario, literally thousands of people are coming to the churches seeking God. Specifically, Elim has received 11,366 new attenders since these two earthquakes hit

San Salvador. The new believers were easily absorbed into the cells of the church. Further, due to the lack of seats in Elim's worship center which holds 5,400 chairs, various sections of the church are worshiping on different days of the week. An explosion of salvations, cells and Celebration services were experienced by these ready saints at Elim.

Let's face the facts! In many churches, a heavy thunderstorm or a few inches of snow may halt the corporate gathering. Not so with the people of Elim church. Why? Because they are structured to be responsive to the needs of others consistently looking to live out the Great Commandment and the Great Commission. The structure is infused with values like sacrifice, love and commitment to Christ's call to see El Salvador and beyond experience a touch from God.

Is your church structure sleek, trim, well-groomed, and amenable? Are you ready for a natural disaster or community crisis? Are you ready to receive God's harvest that we know is coming? Let's be a church that is prepared, proactive, and "on the scene." Paul's word of encouragement to Pastor Timothy rings in my ears, *"Preach the Word; be prepared in season and out of season..." (2 Timothy 4:2a).*

Your church's readiness and preparation begin with your values. Do you value a pristine, ever so polished image in which everything and everyone looks dapper and apropos? Or, do you value God's power, his grace, his Word and love in your midst? I encourage you to establish a few core values which will serve as a small set of guiding principles for your church. These values will be the organism's essential and enduring tenets and should not be confused with specific cultural or operating practices. Further, these values are not to be compromised for financial gain or short term expediency.[77] CCC's core values are as follows:

- We adhere to the eternal authority and relevance of the scripture *(2 Timothy 3:16; Psalm 119:105, 160; Psalm 12:6).*

- We are Christ-centered because Christ is Lord *(John 1:1-5, 12, 14; John 3:16-17; Hebrews 4:14-15).*

- All members are equipped and engaged for the work of service *(2 Timothy 2:2; Ephesians 4:11-13).*

These core values are stakes in the ground that will endure through the ages providing a rudder to steer the church's course upon the open sea. These core values help us to capture the essence of our existence or our purpose (a set of fundamental reasons for existence not to be confused with specific goals or strategies). CCC's purpose is as follows:

Nothing is impossible with God; therefore, CCC is to become a loving, accepting, forgiving FAMILY, united in the purpose of actively:

❦ Celebrating God's Presence   ❦ Equipping God's People

❦ Communicating God's Word   ❦ Demonstrating God's Love

Empowered by the Spirit of God to exemplify the lifestyle of Jesus Christ and His mission to others.

CCC's purpose grows from the root of our core values and leads us to pursue this vision: "Building a Community, Changing a City, Reaching and Country (and world)." The troopers at CCC know this vision. Pastor Eddie has put these words to a worship tune that we sing during Celebration services. Frankly, some of our members can't remember the vision statement by just reciting the words, but they can sing it!

Although there is always room for improvement in the structure of the church, I want to share how the clarification of values, purpose and vision can free a church body to pursue challenging opportunities.

It was a quiet Sunday afternoon at my house. Finding a few minutes to brush up on a teaching for our leadership community to be given that very night, I received a phone call from Carl Galyon and Carl Horton of Church Dynamics International. They were in a pinch and needed some assistance. A ministry trip to Indonesia had been scheduled and they desperately needed a woman to journey with them to help equip pastors' wives in that region of the world. I communicated to these gentlemen that I didn't know what we could do in such a short time frame (the ministry team would leave in two weeks), but that I would present it to the leadership community and see if God would move any of our ladies to fill the gap. I announced the opportunity to our leaders and asked any woman who might be led of God to talk with me at the conclusion of the gathering. Two women responded. One of the ladies was Amy, a sprite young married woman with an eye for adventure. Amy and her husband shepherd a cell and both have been equipped in the discipleship strategy that were to be presented to the churches in Indonesia. Amy had accompanied a previous team of ministers from CCC to Zimbabwe and this journey birthed in her a heart for cross-cultural missions. To make a long story short, Amy voyaged to Indonesia and was a tremendous asset to the ministry of CDI in this country.

When the leaders of CDI learned that CCC was able to help, they were stunned and overjoyed at this rapid response. This type of response may seem impulsive to many. I would disagree. While one must contemplate the risks of deploying to a dangerous part of the globe, this response was a result of knowing the values, purpose and vision of the church. In other words, we are structured in such a way to accomplish our one word primary result—send. In the years and months previous to this experience for Amy, the body equipped her to be ready at any moment. When she sensed God's call, she responded. God confirmed his call by assembling the monies needed for this trip and granting to Amy, a willing and available servant, great fruit in a distant land.

I have written previously of my dear friend from Zimbabwe, Patrick Mpande. I will not soon forget a conversation I had with Patrick during my third visit to his country while driving from his hometown of Redcliffe to the nation's capital of Harare. I had noticed that the various churches that he had planted in Zimbabwe revolved around his personality, vision, passion and fabulous leadership skills. Yet, I did not say anything to Patrick. I observed him answering unending phone calls and running continual errands while simultaneously trying to pastor a growing church and lead his own family. On this day, Patrick began our conversation. "Rob, I'm tired. Everything revolves around me. I am the hub in the middle of the wheel. Nothing goes forward without me. It seems as if I would die, then the ministry would cease to exist." I smiled and let him continue. I listened to him for at least one hour. I hurt for him. This is a man who has a gigantic heart for God and his country. I sensed God was ready to show up in that rented SUV—and He did.

Humbly, I granted to Patrick care and comfort. I praised him for being an incredible man after God's own heart. I encouraged him to ponder the structure of the twenty-six churches that he planted. I made some observations based on my previous visits to the churches in this exotic land. By the end of our dialogue, God spoke to Patrick and he has never been the same. He determined that he must empower his people, stop trying to be everything to everybody, and transition to cell life and cell structure. This is exactly what Patrick did. Can you imagine Patrick's surprise upon returning to Zimbabwe after a six month absence (raising funds in the States and the UK) and learning that the church he pastors doubled in size due to the multiplication of healthy, life-giving cells?

Because of this one decision concerning the structure of the church, God has now multiplied out a dynamic team from the Zimbabwe churches to plant churches in the UK and Europe. Who comprises this team? Yes, Patrick and his family. God has pulled back the curtain for Patrick and revealed to him a vision to reach an additional region of the world. The churches of Zimbabwe are to be commended for they sent their very best—Patrick and Gladys Mpande and family! Truly, the structure of your church can be a blessing or a great hindrance to God's continual call upon your life. Let's investigate church structure in more breadth and depth right now!

I owe a great amount of gratitude to Pastor Rick Warren for his excellent work in the context of church structure not only at Saddleback Community Church, but throughout the world. As a young, youth pastor, I had the opportunity to address the youth of Saddleback and investigate the structure of this powerful church. I want to share some insights that Pastor Rick has taught me and many others concerning establishing a life-giving structure in a church.

Jesus is described as the new wine. A cell structure, small group structure, meta-church structure, or traditional program based design is merely a wine skin. I bless a myriad of church structures. God has led me, however, to pursue leading and planting cell churches throughout the world. My reasons are numerous and will be clearly understood when you read the "Stories of Life" chapter in this book.

An often heard portion of scripture which deals with pouring new wine into old wineskins is found in *Mark 2:18-22*. I cringe when I hear presenters of the gospel use this metaphor of Jesus as a proof text for a specific type of structure for a church. I do not believe that this is the intent of this passage of scripture. The context of this passage of scripture centers in on the Pharisees questioning Jesus concerning the practice of fasting. During this time, fasting was a spiritual discipline linked to mourning. The law commanded the Jews to fast once a year during the Day of Atonement. The Pharisees clothed in their own self righteousness, however, demanded that people fast twice a week. This display of religion was dramatized and publicized by the Pharisees whitening their faces and shredding their robes. I will not use this passage as justification for a particular form of church structure.

I am willing, however, to extract some principles from this confrontation between the Pharisees and Jesus in order to lay a foundation for "new wine societies" in contrast with "old bags." Let me explain. Indeed, Jesus is the new wine which includes the gospel and his Spirit. The new wineskins are those who have received the new wine (personally and corporately). Jesus is making the following point: "The old wineskins of relating to God through religious rules can no longer contain the new wine." Jesus is calling for new wine societies to proclaim him as head, make the word of God their foundation, and embrace and experience the Spirit of God. These new wine societies can be described in the following two ways.

First, a new wine society is teeming with life. *"For whoever finds me finds life" (Proverbs 8:35)*. This means that this society is continually and consistently focused on adding new lives into the kingdom. Do you know that a church will experience new life when new lives are added to the body? A society teeming with life emphasizes life giving relationships. My friend, Jim Roddie, has the reputation in my town of being a fabulous producer of home grown tomatoes. In years past, Jim has taken me through his garden showing me how to meticulously care for these tomato plants. One day, he pointed to an outgrowth from the vine of a tomato plant and asked, "Pastor Rob, do you know what that is right there?" I made up some foolish answer and he smiled and chuckled. He continued, "Rob, that there is a sucker. It looks like it will produce a good fruit, but it won't. We've got to cut off those suckers. They're not good for the plant and won't produce good tomatoes." Being a preacher and writer in the constant pursuit of a good illustration, I took hold of this experience with Jim. I want to grant life in my relationships. I want to teem with new life. I don't want to be a sucker to God and my fellow man.

Second, a new wine society prays against the seducing power of the spirit of religion. A religious spirit can be described in many ways, but let me offer some characteristics of such a spirit. As I begin to unpack these characteristics, please remember the context of this scriptural text. Jesus is bringing to light how a good and right spiritual discipline has been deceitfully turned into a religious practice void of life and meaning. Keeping this in mind, a religious spirit caresses a sense that one is closer to God than other people and/or that his/her life and ministry is more pleasing to God. The root of this sense is obviously pride and it sounds like, "We've got our stuff together." Another sign of a religious spirit is manifested in a person that is always trying to fix what's wrong with other people as if they were appointed by God. The root of this manifestation is judgment and it sounds like, "When will you ever be more like me?" Inflexibility laced with legalism and an enticement with perfectionism rounds out the field for one who embodies a religious spirit.

Moreover, Jesus is exposing the "old bags" of religion—the Pharisees. He is reminding them that the old was based on the Law of Moses; the new is based on him. The old required perfection in its followers; the new requires faith in Christ's perfection. The old was earned through observing its tenets; the new is a free gift of God's grace received through man's faith. The old glorified the keeper of the Law; the new glorifies God and his Son. The old was impossible to attain; the new is freely available to all. The old produced frustration and bondage; the new produces assurance and freedom.

To summarize, the wine is new. The blood is shed. The punishment for our sins is executed. Death is defeated. The bridegroom is risen. The Spirit is sent. The wine is new. The old bag mindset is simply not adequate.[78] What is your desire—to experience the new wine society—the living church of Jesus Christ, or to be an old bag?

Did you know that in Jesus' time that old wineskins could be made new? The restoration process entailed placing the old wineskin (which really was a goat skin) in a vat of oil. The vat of oil including the wineskin would then be hung in a tree allowing the breeze to penetrate the wineskin with the permeating oil. This process produced a skin that was soft, supple and pliable. Do the principles squeezed from *Mark 2:18-22* cause you to ask God for fresh oil and wind in your church? Let's consider now a lesson from the animal world.

No animal can grow more than nine inches in height without a skeletal system. For the animal, this skeletal system provides an organized structure for growth. Churches also need a structure that will enable growth to occur. Many churches struggle because their structure limits their growth. When a church's structure is not adequate, members may begin to fight over certain decisions causing internal conflict. Furthermore, a poor church structure can produce fatigue and low morale in key leaders. It is important to note that structure does not cause growth, but it does control the rate and size of growth.

Upon close investigation, one will find that no two human skeletal systems are identical. A skeletal system (or structure) for a church can also be quite unique. The nature of a church determines its structure whether it be traditional or non-traditional. Because the church is considered a living organism (not an organization), structure that retards growth is unwarranted for any church. Read this last sentence once again. Why would any church adhere to a structure that paralyzes the church to minister?

Think of the following words: Committee, Majority Rule, Vote, Officers, Board, Business Meeting, Elections, Ballot, Democracy. What do these words have in common?

Answer: None of these are New Testament concepts of church

structure. They are <u>American</u> concepts. These forms of church structure lend themselves to create conflict instead of harmony. In developing Biblical structures for church life, we must be good at asking the right questions. Here are some questions for you to consider: What kind of structure is best to reach the unchurched where they are and help them grow to maturity so they too can become ministers? What kind of structure will allow Christians to grow in maturity and responsibility while meeting their needs? What is this church really about? What are our goals? Who is Christ asking us to reach, teach and equip? Does your church structure reflect the values of your church?

As I have stated already, the nature of the church determines its structure. Here are some things to ponder rooted in the scriptures concerning the church's nature. First, the church is a family. *"You should be like one big, happy family, full of sympathy toward each other, loving one another with tender hearts and humble minds" (I Peter 3:8, LB).* God desires that we operate on the basis of *relationships* not *regulations*. In a family, the *mature* lead. The most responsible are to lead out by modeling and teaching the younger members of the family. *1 Timothy 3:4-5* and *5:1-2* teach us that leaders are to display excellence in the relationship that they have with their own families.

Second, the church is a fellowship. *Acts 2:42 (PH)* describes the early church: *"They continued steadily learning the teaching of the apostles and joined in the fellowship."* A top priority in a fellowship is intimacy and unity. *"Make every effort to keep the unity of the Spirit through the bond of peace" (Ephesians 4:3). John 17:23* teaches us that any attitude that causes disunity is sin in the eyes of God. A life-giving structure promotes unity and downplays differences. Have you ever gone to a church meeting and walked away wondering why you attended in the first place? I have. This is not a new phenomenon. The Apostle Paul wrote to the church in Corinth, *"(Often)...your meetings do more harm than good because I hear that when you come together as a church, there are <u>divisions among you</u>..." (I Corinthians 11:17-18).*

Third, the church is a body. *(See I Corinthians 12:27, Ephesians 1:22-23; 5:23, Colossians 1:18; 2:19).* God has granted to each body member spiritual gifts; therefore, we function on the basis of spiritual gifts, not elected office. Voting in the church will eventually divide the body members. When I lift myself out of bed in the morning, I don't vote for my physical body parts to function as they do, it's their gift. The church is not looking for people who want a title. Jesus wants servants who are gifted by God. Please also understand that there is a great difference between an organization and an organism (or body). An organization emphasizes maintenance, but an organism focuses on ministry. Develop a simple structure that maximizes ministry and minimizes maintenance.

Jesus' favorite description of the church will help your church develop a purposeful structure. The church is a flock *(John 10:1-30, Matthew 25:33; 26:31)*. Because the church is a flock, it is cared for and led by shepherds. *"Jesus asked Simon Peter, `Do you really love me?' `Yes Lord,' said Peter, `Then take care of my sheep'"* *(John 21:16-17)*. As I have already articulated in this book, we must unleash the people as "ministers." The pastors and shepherds are the "equippers." Is this biblical, my friends? You bet! *"And He gave some as apostles, and some as prophets, and some as evangelists, and some as pastors and teachers, for the equipping of the saints for the work of service, to the building up of the body of Christ" (Ephesians 4:11-12).*

A practical example may help. I penned the majority of these chapters in this book while on a ten week sabbatical from my responsibilities as pastoral team leader at CCC. Over the past 10 years, God has built an outstanding leadership team of overseers, pastors and shepherds. During my sabbatical, this team handled everything with immense dedication, focus and skill. The church body contributed their gifts of worship, counseling, teaching and more in a steadfast pursuit of CCC's vision. I have had no concerns with the adequacy of these individuals. Pastor, what would a sabbatical look like for you? Has God graced you with a deep bench? Are others equipped to do what you do? If not, then you may have some structural damage that needs to be addressed. Once again, the church is a family, a fellowship, a body, and a flock. Does your church structure support the nature of the church that we find in scripture?

Through the reading of this chapter, I trust that you are connecting the dots. I have stated that the foundation of the church's structure begins with understanding your core values. Aligning everything that you do with these three to five core values is necessary and essential. These core values help us to capture the essence of our existence, our purpose. Our purpose leads us to pursue a common vision which keeps us on course through life's journey. Finally, our people long to experience being in a family, to fellowship with each other, employing their gifts in the body as we follow the Chief Shepherd.

I began this chapter arguing against a rigid structure that sucks the life out of the church. As you know, there is another extreme that can be just as frustrating. Obviously, it is a church body that deems herself to be quite spiritual because of the lack of structure. In other words, there are a lot of whistles blowing and the boiler is a stirrin', but there is little evidence of life change, multiplication and fruitfulness. Maybe a word picture would better help communicate this dilemma in the context of functional structures.

In this part of the country, an assortment of rivers and creeks flow through the Hill Country of Texas. These picturesque waters have one thing in common. The waters are girded in by banks on each side. The banks exist for a variety of reasons including flood control, direction of the flow of water, and accessibility to the water which is a high value to this region. Now, picture the curious swamps that fill the states such as Florida and Louisiana. While they can be a sportsman's paradise, they are largely void of banks. Specifically, the water flow is multi-directional. Further, it is a simple task to be lost in a swamp. I believe you are catching the significance of some form of life-giving structure in your church.

Does your church have appropriate banks? Do you sense that the stated values, purpose and vision of your church are churning around in swampy waters? Are you "on course" going with the flow of the waters? Are you lost in the dangerous waters filled with gators, crocks and snakes? Are you "straining at the oars" consistently battling the water's currents? Are you moving fast but not going anywhere? Let me state the obvious—your church's alignment encompassing the core values, purpose and vision are paramount in the quest for a life-giving church.

What is one to do? Let's go to the links for a plausible answer.

After a particularly poor game of golf, a popular club member skipped the clubhouse and started to go home. As he was walking to the parking lot to get his car, a policeman stopped him and asked, "Did you tee off on the sixteenth hole about twenty minutes ago?" "Yes," the golfer responded. "Did you happen to hook your ball so that it went over the trees and off the course?" "Yes, I did. How did you know?" he asked. "Well," said the policeman very seriously, "Your ball flew out onto the highway and crashed through a driver's windshield. The car went out of control, crashing into five other cars and a fire truck. The fire truck couldn't make it to the fire, and the building burned down. So, what are you going to do about it?" The golfer thought it over carefully and responded, "I think I'll close my stance a little bit, tighten my grip, and lower my right thumb."

How many churches go about tweaking their structure with blatant disregard for others (those in the body and those who need Christ's body)? Many pastors and leaders shoot themselves in the foot with their constant shifting of values, purpose and vision. As a result, the congregants pay little attention to the "State of the Church Address," the vision inscribed on the church's walls and bulletin, and the policy and procedures for "doing" church. The members don't get excited about new plans. They simply hold on for the ride knowing that the primary leader or leaders will change course quickly. It is a battle over control and direction in which the most stubborn "wins."

My friend, Robert Mearns, reminds the many leaders he works with that "structure" and "life" are not opposites. He teaches that biological research reveals that dead matter and living organisms are not distinguished by their substance, but by the specific *structure* of the relationship of the individual parts to each other. In God's creation, the living and nonliving are formed from identical material substances and are distinguished only by their structure. To further understand this reality, one must consider if a church's structure is considered rigid, redundant and/or religious. Robert encourages the churches that he works with to be radical, reproductive and relevant.

Christian Schwarz crystallizes this thought pattern by writing,

A girl once asked her mother: "Why do you always cut the end of the roast, then lay that end on top before you put it into the oven?" The mother only to admit: "I learned that from your grandmother. I don't know why she did that. But I will ask her." A short time later her opportunity came. "Tell me why did you always cut the end of the roast and lay that end on top of the roast before putting it into the oven?" The grandmother answered: "Don't you remember how small our oven was? That big Sunday roast just did not fit in one piece."

Some things are quite meaningful and appropriate, that is, functional, at a certain point in time. But when the situation changes (and our behavior does not change at the same time) the formerly functional can rapidly develop into something anachronistic or even strange.

Our churches suffer from both: structures, activities, and measures that were meaningful earlier but are no longer because the situation has changed. At the same time there are structures, activities, and measures that have never been functional because they were designed from the beginning in such a way that they never could be fruitful.[79]

As you ponder the parables, scriptures, principles and questions presented in this chapter, let me propose one final question. Are there whistles impeding the body's boiler from moving you downstream in the pursuit of God's given values, purpose and vision in your church? Now is the time to ask God to breathe new life through your church's structure. *"Behold, I am doing a new thing..."*

Chapter Eight

"Life Transformation"
(Inspiring Worship &
Passionate Spirituality)

YOU GOTTA DANCE....

The ***Bolero*** is the slowest of the Latin dances. With passion pouring out of every step, ***Bolero*** is a dance with immense bravado. The moves are long, sweeping; the Latin style is stretched to the limit. This dance is powerfully suggestive and sure to stir your blood. So should it be with our inspiring worship and passionate spirituality.

DANCE WITH ME, DADDY...

Agalliao [Greek]: to jump for joy, to be exceedingly glad or joyful, much leaping.

*"Though you have not seen him, you love him; and even though you do not see him now, you believe in him and are filled with an **inexpressible and glorious joy**" (I Peter 1:8).*

*"Let us **rejoice and be glad** and give him glory! For the wedding of the Lamb has come, and his bride has made herself ready. Fine linen, bright and clean, was given her to wear" (Revelation 19:7-8).*

INTRODUCTION
(by Cecilia Belvin, Prayer/Network Pastor, CCC)

What is this *eagerness to throw off* everything that hinders and the sin that so easily entangles; what fuels *the passion to run with perseverance* the race marked out for us; how do *we come to* Mount Zion, the city of the living God; how do we *will to keep* on *loving* each other as brothers and sisters; how do we *not forget* to entertain strangers; how do *we remember* those in prison as if we were fellow prisoners; how is the marriage bed *kept pure*; how *do we obey* our leaders and *submit* to those in authority; how do we see to it that we *do not refuse Him* who speaks; how do we *continually offer to God a sacrifice* of praise; what enables us *to hold unswervingly* to the hope we profess; how do we continue *to advance* a kingdom that cannot be shaken? *(Hebrews 12 & 13)*

Sounds like passionate spirituality to me!

She is in her seventies but her energy amazes me. She pastors with excellence, poise, and authority in an energetic, ever growing network of cells and leaders while still gracefully caring for a loving husband. She invokes purposed interest in her two daughters and their husbands, and meticulously watches over her numerous devoted grandchildren, who know without a doubt that their grandmother is intensely interested in everything that touches their lives.

Over the past nine years, I have observed her determination to live out the admonishments of *Hebrews 12 and 13*. Her home has been a refuge for strangers...her resources spread far and wide. Her name is Kathryn. She is one passionately spiritual lady!

How does she do it? Because her love for Jesus runs deep...she "remains" in His love.

"I am the true vine...Remain in me, and I will remain in you. No branch can bear fruit by itself; it must remain in the vine. I am the vine...apart from me you can do nothing...Now remain in my love." (John 15)

Passionate spirituality! Remaining in the vine!
Remain by listening and talking to Jesus...intimate prayer.
Remain by meeting Him in His word...knowing Him.
Remain by obedience...yes, Lord.
Remain by utter dependence...nothing apart from the true vine.
The "remaining" produces passionate spirituality that bears much fruit...our Kathryn.

"I surrender to your call upon my heart..."
"I am captured by your desire..."
"You did not die that I could stand idly by..."
Dream CD, Electromotive Worship Project

INTRODUCTION
(by Grayson Belvin, College Network Pastor/Worship Leader, CCC)

Church life hinges on the presence of God. It is in this presence that church methods and techniques come into their finest, playing the supportive parts to the King's leading role. This is why we worship together...because God is perfectly faithful to inhabit the praises of His people. In His presence, he brings the "electricity" that leaves no attending soul unchanged.

Through worship, we are introduced to the person of God and are reminded of the purposes in God. We remember for whom we live this life, and why we live it. We are re-centered by the touch of a loving and powerful King, and we can then go and live and breathe for Him.

And, how we need Him. Outside of the Lord's personal touch, there is absolutely nothing that can sustain the church. An antithesis of worship is self-reliance; worship, on the other hand, says "God we're thinking about you, we love and need You." God, in His unwavering love, always responds with something like, "I've been thinking about you too, and I love you. Be blessed." And we are! Every single time.

We worship because we get to touch God with our love. And, to be completely honest, we worship because He always touches us back. It's from this touch that we can go out and minister with renewed perspective.

Where were you the last time you encountered a life transforming experience? Maybe it was the delivery room as your new addition breathed her first breath. Maybe it was over a great cup of coffee at the local java joint with a colleague or good friend. You may have had this experience over a candlelight dinner with your spouse or in bed with your child answering one of those big questions about life. Some experiences descend upon us during times of solitude with a serendipitous splash that rocks our world. The transformational moment occurred in your deer blind or your Chevy Suburban. Where were you when you had this phenomenal experience—an experience that indeed transformed your life? Unfortunately, the last place anyone today expects to have such an experience is in church. The majority of worship experiences in churches throughout the land are rote, trite, and down right boring, not to mention very predictable. Could this be one reason why the multitudes flock to brew pubs, sporting events and Internet cafes in lieu of worship centers or cell gatherings?

During my recent sabbatical, I had the opportunity to experience thirteen different corporate worship gatherings in six different countries. This experience was eye opening. I discovered what I'm sure you already know. The style of music (contemporary vs. traditional), denominational tag (Baptist, Methodist, Presbyterian, Nondenominational), and physical structure of the building (opulent edifice, dingy shack, water drenched tent, make shift store front) are not the key elements to one experiencing life transformation through inspiring worship. "When the focus [of our worship] shifts from meaning to method, we become modern-day Pharisees."[80] Life transformation is experienced when personal and corporate passionate spirituality preludes inspiring worship.

For clarity sake, let me briefly define "inspiring worship." The root word for "inspiring" is *'inspiratio'*—an inspiredness which comes from the Spirit of God. You see, God places the desire in you to worship him through his Spirit. In essence, you partner with God in worshiping him, but he is the catalyst. 'Worship' can be defined in an unlimited assortment of ways. Indeed, worship is an intense love and adoration for God. Worship involves both attitudes (awe, reverence, respect) as well as actions (bowing, praising, serving). Worship is the response of all that man is to all that God is and does. It is the outward expression of our inward impression of God. For the purpose of this discussion, let me present the following definition of worship. Worship is our individual and corporate response to God's revelation of himself within the context of a covenant relationship. Do you see the word 'relationship?' This is a key component of our worship to God for when there is no relationship, there is no worship. How can we experience inspiring worship? Well, hold on for the ride as we journey down this road.

Let's contemplate the truth that when *"Jesus is lifted up all men will be drawn to him" (John 12:32)*. The prophet Isaiah experienced this truth according to John as he writes, *"Isaiah said [these things] because he saw Jesus' glory and spoke about him" (John 12:41)*. What did Isaiah say as he looked upon the pre-incarnate Christ? He exclaims, *"Holy, Holy, Holy is the Lord of hosts, the whole earth is full of his glory" (Isaiah 6:3)*. This experience with Christ led to transformation in Isaiah's life. As Isaiah cried out to Christ, one of the Seraphim took a hot coal from the altar of the temple and touched it to Isaiah's mouth. The Seraphim stated, *"See, this has touched your lips; your guilt is taken away and your sin atoned for" (Isaiah 6:7)*. What is Isaiah's response? He says to the Lord, "Sign me up, Lord. Send me." Do you see the power of worship and life transformation in Isaiah's encounter with Jesus? Certainly, we might categorize this as inspiring worship! Yet, stories of life transformation are few and far between in the context of worship. Is Jesus being lifted up in our worship gatherings? How can we experience afresh and anew the fabulous glory of Christ? A few stories may help as we consider inspiring worship.

Several years ago, I was moved by God and recruited by others to help out a good friend who was close to divorcing his wife. My friend lived in the Dallas area and I invited him to join me at a Promise Keepers event at Texas Stadium. A large contingency of men from CCC were headed north for this event and it seemed natural to include my good buddy. Being a nominal Christian man, my friend gladly accepted my invitation. I was surprised and grateful. I began praying for a breakthrough in his life. For nearly two days he (along with thousands of other men) was immersed in the very real presence of God. I wept as I saw him weep kneeling beside his stadium seat. Yet, I wasn't quite sure what God was up to in this man's heart.

As we pulled away from the stadium, I tentatively and gently asked him, "Well, what do you think? How was all of that for you?" He responded with one word, "Passion." I wasn't sure if I heard his response and I asked, "What did you say?" "I said—passion," he replied. "What do you mean?" I inquired. Slowly, my friend unfolded the following broken phrases, "The passion was....[long pause] unbelievable...amazing...[his voice began to quiver]...Those men are on fire....I don't have that but I loved it....Every part of it....That's what's wrong with church today, Rob—it's the lack of passion. Hell, there is no passion for God in my church!"

Recently, a man who I would describe as "over churched" entered the worship center at CCC to experience a Celebration gathering. I had the opportunity to meet this gentleman a few weeks after this initial visit and as is my habit, I asked him, "Tell me about your experience at CCC's Celebration." With a slight grin on his face and his head moving back and forth slightly, he spoke. "Well," he said, "as the service progressed, I conjured up every reason to find the door and make a quick exit. The music was loud, the kids with an assorted variety of colors on their heads were hopping around, the dancers were a dancin,' and the flags were whippin' around my head and my wife's head and...let's just say that it was "different." So, in my mind, I planned my exit strategy. Then something happened. People began coming to the altar, kneeling down, praying to God. Some were weeping. This was weird for me because the worship leader didn't ask for this response—it just happened. Eventually, during this time of worship, the altar was filled with individuals being prayed for by the—I don't know who they were—maybe the cell group shepherds?? At any rate, I was moved and moved deeply. The spirit and excitement were contagious and I knew this was okay, right, and moving. But the most important thing that I realized is that I experienced Christ in a new and fresh way."

To repeat, passionate spirituality (personally and corporately) preludes inspiring worship. The heart of passionate spirituality is intercession. John Wesley once said, "God will do nothing on earth except in answer to believing prayer." Think of Christ's powerful modeling of prayer while here on earth. Let me paint a picture for you.

You see Christ hugging the blood stained rock nestled among the gnarly roots of the olive trees in the Garden of Gethsemane. His prayer shawl is covering his head and his dark hair splashes onto his shoulders. He is praying. You are listening in on his prayers. As you inch toward Christ, you hear your name! The Lord of Lords, the King of Kings, the Creator, the Lamb of God is praying for you. You are humbled, shocked and filled with awe and gratitude. Christ is praying for you! Now, that would be an incredible experience, would it not? You bet. He still is praying for you—as your chief intercessor and great advocate even now. Is the church today guilty of substituting stylistic techniques, articulate messages and technological razzle-dazzle for the eternal power of intercession? This is my deeply held belief. I wonder what would happen if our worship leaders and pastors spent equal time in prayer for the worship gathering as they do preparing nice songs and messages. I know that more and more people would experience life transformation.

One poignant message of Christ's prayer for you in the garden is this: It is impossible to lose your footing while on your knees. Jesus is our example. His ministry can be described as moving from one house of prayer to the next and in between he worked miracles. The scriptures allow us to see life transformation meshed with the power of prayer and intercession in *Matthew 21:12-16*. Here, Jesus declares the temple as a house of prayer, not a den of thieves. This declaration is meshed with the cleansing of the temple. Jesus is saying, "Not only is the temple a house of prayer, but also a house of purity." Do you know it is a good thing when Jesus cleanses the temple? Further, the blind and the lame rush to Jesus and are healed. Those gathered experience the power of Christ. At this point please notice the indignation of the chief priests. Their anger is not rooted solely in what Jesus is doing, but at the acclamation that he is receiving. The children lead out in a chorus of praise, *"Hosanna to the Son of David."* Praise fills the temple—passionate praise! I mean these children were shouting out praises to Jesus. The house of prayer becomes a house of purity filled with power and praise!

In the context of prayer, I think often of the scriptural command, *"I want men everywhere to lift up holy hands in prayer, without anger or dissension" (I Timothy 2:8).* Pointedly, we are commanded to be free from irritation (no wrath) toward our fellow man. Next, we are to direct our confidence toward God (no dissension or doubting). Prayer is relationship, not a religious activity. We are directed to *"pray continually" (I Thessalonians 5:17a).*

How do you view prayer? You may picture yourself at the throne of God. Here you see his majesty, power and grace. Or, you may see prayer as a walk on a road with an intimate friend. These two pictures present us with a magnificent balance in our lives of prayer.

Prayer is the most tangible trace of eternity in the human heart. We must rely, depend and anchor our hopes for inspiring worship in prayer. Generally, my main role in CCC's worship gatherings is that of teaching. A few years ago, God granted to me two great gifts. The first gift was the agreement of fifty men in the church who committed to praying for me at least once a day. As these men prayed for me, I immediately sensed God's Spirit flow through me in many different and new ways, especially during the times that God allowed me to teach during CCC's Celebrations. This was the second gift that God gave to me. He clearly revealed to me that the power of teaching rests in nothing else but intercession. I completely concur with E.M. Bounds: "Those in the power given to praying for the pastor are like poles which hold up the wires along which the electric current runs. They are not the power, neither are they the specific agents in making the Word of the Lord effective. But they hold up the wires upon which the divine power runs to the hearts of men."[81]

Every week on Saturday night at CCC's physical building in "The Gap" (prayer chapel), various members of the body are praying for God to reveal himself to those who will be present at Celebration services. I am convinced without a shadow of doubt that this is the power that undergirds our worship experience. Further, the prayer ministry teams of CCC are continually lifting up the Celebration and cell gatherings that occur week in and week out. If you want to experience life transformation during your times of worship, then begin with intercession—the root of passionate spirituality.

A look at *Exodus 17:8-16* will further enlighten us as we press into the power of prayer. Here we find Joshua engaged in battle with the enemy and Moses receiving support from Aaron and Hur. Let me point out one principle that will revolutionize your times of worship. The battle in the trenches is necessary and important (this is Joshua's role). However, ultimate victory comes through prayer and intercession (Moses, Aaron, Hur). You see, my friend, the history of the church belongs to the intercessor. In active warfare for the souls of men and women, the most critical information is not what you know, but what you don't know. It is fatal to step into the war zone unaware of where the true battleground is located. Neglecting this intercessory power is a sin against God. Without a continual participation in experiencing intercession we are thumbing our noses at God and saying, "We have this under control. We know how to do this worship thing. We'll ring you when we run into a jam."

I wholeheartedly believe that God can transform the drag and drudgery of worship (in the majority of our churches) to experiences of power and praise. God can turn boredom into exciting experiences filled with fun. John Smith was a key leader in the 1970's when the Jesus Movement hit the land of Australia. This movement targeted wandering seekers and those who felt marginalized and alienated from the established culture. "Irish Christians," Smith says, "See the Kingdom of God in part as a party—where the doors are thrown open like an Irish pub—festive, music, participatory—with everyone welcome. Here, no one is going to check your credentials. Leave your attitude at the door, come in, find your place, and feel free to express your gift."[82] Let it be so for your church and mine! Indeed, a majority of churches have not yet discovered that is okay to make church interesting.

As one intercedes for the worship gatherings (Celebration and/or cell), God works in the hearts of people. Certainly, he will work in our own heart. Yet, there is another element of passionate spirituality that will enhance our corporate times of worship. It is our personal worship to God. The depth of our worship of God will always be in direct proportion to the revelation of God's closeness. *Romans 12:1* reminds us that we worship him with our lives. *"Therefore, I urge you, brothers, in view of God's mercy, to offer your bodies as living sacrifices, holy and pleasing to God—this is your spiritual act of worship." Hebrews 13:15* reads, *"Through Jesus, therefore, let us continually offer to God a sacrifice of praise—the fruit of our lips that confess His name" (Hebrews 13:15).*

Inspiring worship, therefore, is not something that can be

reduced to one or two hours on Sunday morning. God desires our lives to be a continual instrument of worship to Him. Do you remember the definition given earlier in this chapter for worship? Worship is our individual and corporate response to God's revelation of himself within the context of a covenant relationship. Do you see the word 'revelation'? As we experience personal worship, God reveals himself to us and as we gather together in corporate worship—we truly will experience "Celebration." The members of the body of Christ are coming together to celebrate God's activity in our own personal lives.

My assertion is that Christians treat the corporate worship gatherings as they do a drive thru at a fast food restaurant. These bastions of food preparation and delivery exist to get something in your stomach as soon as possible. You drive thru because you don't want to take the time to prepare your own food. Simply put, we favor convenience over the toil of food preparation. Similarly, most Christians are not in the continual and consistent habit of personally receiving from God. They have not caught the savor of his fresh bread which is available each day and provides nourishment for daily living. They are not independently dependent on God, but are dependent upon others to feed them. A worship leader is necessary for them to experience worship. A teacher is central to receiving scriptural principles of life.

We have learned that passionate spirituality preludes inspiring worship. The root of passionate spirituality is intercession. One manifestation of passionate spirituality is our own personal worship of God. We worship him continually with our lives and refuse to treat God and others like a McDonald's or Dairy Queen. As A.W. Tozer explains, "We are called to an everlasting preoccupation with God." Can you picture how your times of corporate Celebrations would be enhanced if each member of the body were continually preoccupied with God?

Now, let's consider the object, place, and expression of the corporate worship experience. Whatever we devote ourselves to (our passion), whatever occupies us (our thoughts, emotions, desires and discussions) will govern the way we live our lives and is ultimately our object of worship. Do you know that many worship—worship? Others worship the church. Jesus says, *"The time is coming and has now come when the true worshipers will worship the Father in spirit and truth, for they are the kind of worshipers the Father seeks" (John 4:23)*. What happens when God finds true worshipers? that person? that church? that congregation? He says, "I will reveal myself to these people." When God reveals himself to you, then you experience *inspiratio*.

Worship takes place within the life of a believer who is in intimate relationship with Christ and living under the control of the Holy Spirit. The place of our worship is not a specific location, but a surrendered heart. The Bible uses the term 'heart' to represent the center of your motivation, desires, and inclinations. My heart determines why I say the things I do. *"The mouth speaks what the heart is full of" (Matthew 12:34, GN)*. My heart determines why I feel the way I do (joy, fear, despair, sorrow, love, hate, jealousy). *"The Word of God...examines the thoughts and motives of the heart" (Hebrews 4:12 PH)*. My heart determines why I act the way I do. *"Guard your heart, for it is the wellspring of life" (Proverbs 4:23)*. The Bible makes it very clear that your heart was designed by God, but you make the choice to use it for good or evil, for selfish purposes or for service. You may have *"selfish ambition in your heart" (James 3:14)* or you may *"serve the Lord with all your heart" (I Samuel 12:20)*.

God desires for us to have a perfect heart. "Wait a minute," you exclaim, "I'll never be perfect." You're right, but you can have a perfect heart. God's idea of a perfect heart is one that is searchable *(Jeremiah 17:10, Psalm 24:3-5)*, trusting *(Proverbs 3:5-6, Psalm 11:1, Psalm 25:1-2)*, and broken *(Psalm 34:18)*. As the psalmist proclaims to God, *"You don't want penance; if you did, how gladly I would do it! You aren't interested in offerings burned before you on the altar. It is a broken spirit you want—remorse and penitence. A broken and a contrite heart, O God, you will not ignore" (Psalm 51:16-17)*. When our object of worship becomes God and him alone, and we experience God working in the place of worship (our heart), then get ready for inspiring worship.

A true, Christ-centered, Spirit-filled inward attitude will determine the outward expression of our worship. Can you place yourself next to Michal (daughter of Saul, see *I Chronicles 15:28-29*) as she despised David in her heart for his worship to God? Can you see her crinkled brow and the venomous glare of her eyes? Can you feel the hatred of the Pharisees as Jesus is being praised as he enters into Jerusalem? (see *Mark 14:3-4).* What expressions do you see during times of corporate worship in your church? Are you inspired or depressed? As you contemplate worship, you discover that worship is a verb. The Bible grants to us many expressions of worship including kneeling, dancing, clapping, shouting, singing, and the lifting of our hands. Let me grant to you a caution concerning one's expression of worship. Your expression of worship is not the only right way to worship God. People who tend to disagree with this caution are usually in the camp of those who worship— worship. They have misappropriated the object of their worship.

Personally, I have experienced inspired worship in a public park in the city of Bogota, Colombia with 40,000 young people complete with band, dancers, lights and a simple, Biblical message on salvation presented by Pastor Cesar Fajardo. I was filled with inspiration as the orchestra and 120 voice choir sang praises to God at Yoido Full Gospel Church in Seoul, South Korea. Further, inspired worship has filled my heart in many homes throughout the world as small groups of believers gathered together in homes with no musical instruments or CD players. I have received inspiration from God through a silent observation of the Lord's Supper at CCC. I have been moved by grade school kids leading a worship tune at CCC for all generations on a Sunday morning in "big church." I have sensed the presence of God in a large tent in Redcliffe, Zimbabwe filled with the deafening volume of an antiquated keyboard and a small choir. To see one thousand men, women, young people, and children dance in circles before God is a sight you will never forget. As a guest at these varied places, I have been inspired through a specific people group's indigenous worship to God. Leonard Sweet writes, "When worship is indigenous, it swells from the waters in which it is brought to life. Indigenous worship is incarnation, not imitation or replication. It is ministry by embodiment, not ministry by mimicry."[83]

I trust my point is clear. Yes, the scriptures grant to us a conglomeration of expressions in the context of worship, but be careful that you do not embrace the dividing attitude of "my way or the highway." This heart attitude is more about you than God. Let us wholeheartedly, therefore, worship God as he desires. If we refuse to participate in this experience, then *"the stones will cry out" (Luke 19:40)* with exaltation and praise to God.

Throughout this chapter, I have repeatedly and deliberately used the word 'experience.' My initial question at the beginning of this chapter asked, "Where were you the last time you encountered a life transforming *experience?*" I would like to round out this chapter by encouraging you to contemplate how you might partner with God in creating such an experience.

As we open our eyes and study what has happened and is happening in the economy and culture, we may learn some things that will stimulate us to act in creating life transforming experiences in our worship gatherings. "Churches in the postmodern communities will be built; not around great preachers, but around great experiences. Preaching must cease to be the 'big-jug/little-jugs' presentation of points of view or the representation of arguments that can be verbalized; rather, it must become a rushing mighty wind that blows through the congregation and makes it glow with an incandescence that cannot be ignored."[84] "In fact, for worship in the 21st century," write Bill Easum and Thomas Bandy, "If you can say it all with words, you've missed the point!"[85] We live in an "experience economy" and can now partner with God to help turn the tide of boring, lifeless, trite worship.

"In the course of my lifetime," writes B. Joseph Pine, "The world has moved from an 'industrial economy' to a 'service economy' to an 'experience economy.' "[86] John Naisbitt, who coined the term "experience economy," explains:

> Economic activity starts with *raw commodities* that are transformed into *goods*, which are then wrapped in *services* and eventually turned into *experiences*. Each level increases the total value to the customer and, therefore, the total price...A cup of coffee requires about a penny's worth of coffee beans (the *raw commodity*) and about a nickel's worth of coffee grounds (a packaged

good). If you purchase a cup of coffee at a diner, though, you will pay around 50 cents for the *service*, and, at a fine restaurant, as much as $2 to $3 for the *experience*.[87]

To actualize the above rationale, think of the difference between pouring yourself a cup of coffee at your local convenience store or savoring a cup of java and the conversation at your local Starbucks. 7-11 is providing you a service; Starbucks an experience. If you lack the vision for this, then venture to the downtown Starbucks in Seoul, South Korea, Seattle, Washington, Los Angeles, California, or Austin, Texas where you will find hundreds of Gen-Xers, business colleagues, and families gathered around small tables having the time of their lives. They are experiencing one another and life over their $3.50 Café Mocha. Starbucks around the world, my friend, is cashing in on the "experience economy." Pine and Gilmore grant further clarification:

> So depending on what a business does with it, coffee can be any of three economic offerings—commodity, good, or service—with three distinct ranges of value customers attach to the offering. But wait: Serve that same coffee in a five-star restaurant or espresso bar, where the ordering, creation, and consumption of the cup embodies a heightened ambience or sense of theatre, and consumers gladly part anywhere from $2 to $5 for each cup. Businesses that ascend to this fourth level of value establish a distinctive experience that envelops the purchase of coffee, increasing its value (and therefore its price) by two orders of magnitude over the original commodity.[88]

People today are paying top dollar for experiences. Consider the awesome experience of shopping at Bass Pro Shops Outdoor World, REI (Recreational Equipment, Inc), Cabela's World Headquarters, or Seattle's Nike Town; or eating at the Rainforest Café surrounded by the sounds of animals, waterfalls, and calls of the wild. The "experience economy" has revolutionized even how we give gifts to each other. Although a Tommy Hilfiger shirt is nice to receive, many individuals would opt for symphony tickets, a ski trip, or tickets to the local cinema.

This quest for experience may frighten you as you center in on the obvious—one's emotional state should not dictate eternal truths about God and/or worship. This declaration is certainly valid, but should not deter us from capitalizing on the depth and breadth of this cultural phenomenon. "A continental drift of the soul has taken place whereby spirituality is less creedal, less propositional, more relational, and more sensory."[89] What an awesome opportunity is before us; partnering with God to create life transforming experiences for others.

Have you ever been on a "Walk to Emmaus?" This experiential retreat provided by Methodist churches throughout the country is quite a journey capitalizing on the power of the Lord's Supper and the element of surprise. For the most part, today's corporate worship gatherings are void of symbolism and the mystical. Additionally, being "surprised" during worship is a "laugher." Most congregants would be dismayed not to find an order of worship in their bulletin. Pastors do not spend enough time in meditation and solitude which births creativity, "thinking outside the box," and presenting with flair the resurrected Christ. Let me center in on this element of surprise.

In the context of the experience economy, Pine and Gilmore display the following formula: Customer surprise = What a customer gets to perceive minus What a customer expects to get. Rather than merely meeting expectations or setting new ones, companies deliberately try to transcend expectations and go off in new directions entirely. Simply put, it is when a company purposively stages the unexpected.[90] As a pastor, I will be the first to admit that this requires work as we consider the nuances of inspiring worship. But, as I have encouraged you before—open your eyes and look around you. The goal is not to be original, but adaptive in partnering with God for life transforming experiences.

As an example, I have been working in recent days with the three primary worship leaders at CCC. We are in the midst of a God-given transition. Our primary worship leader for the last seven years is being multiplied out to a nearby town to plant a church.

Pastor Eddie is a wonderful worship leader, but an even better mentor and teacher of leading others in worship. Specifically, over the last few years, Eddie has "groomed," encouraged, and challenged dozens of individuals who lead and participate on CCC's worship teams. During this transition, I have become the key person for CCC's Celebration gatherings. Please understand that my musical talents are minimal. I am not gifted to lead worship, but thanks to God and Eddie, I am one member of a team that can partner with God to create life transforming experiences.

At a recent gathering with these three worship leaders, I proposed the following two questions: What is God asking us to experience during our times of Celebration? How do we get there? The responses to these questions were predictable as we began the fascinating journey of creating experiences for God to reveal himself and for people to experience the living Christ. For this team, the inspiring worship experience begins the moment their feet hit the asphalt upon parking their vehicle (I should not forget to remind you of the passionate spirituality elements before mentioned in this chapter. I am concentrating now on aesthetics and environment). As the worshipers ease their way into the Worship Center that we call the "Living Room," the rocks are crying out with praise and worship to God—literally. You see, we made an investment in good quality speakers that are disguised as rocks. The music is subtle, yet powerful. You should see the inquisitive kids trying to figure out the source of the music. On one Sunday morning, a bright nine-year-old boy exclaimed, "See Mom—I told you the rocks were singing." We are partnering with God in preparing one's heart for worship through rocks that sing!

Although I brought this idea to the table, in no way is it original. I borrowed (precise use of words—I might say 'stole') the idea from SeaWorld, Six Flags, and DisneyWorld. Upon a recent journey with my family to one of these entertainment parks, I began singing along with the music in the parking lot. Then I thought, "Where is the music coming from?" Well, the music is everywhere—in the parking lots, on the trolleys, in the bathrooms. It is no wonder we can't get the tune of "It's a Small World" out of our minds after such an excursion. Do you know that I have watched the people who attend Celebration at CCC humming and singing to the music hundreds of yards from the "Living Room?" God is preparing their hearts through singing rocks.

Please understand that investing in singing rocks will not insure that inspiring worship will take place in your church. The worship team leaders that I am honored to lead are looking at the worship gathering through the lens of experience. Further, do you know where I am minutes prior to our Celebration services? I'm listening to the singing rocks, shaking hands, and giving hugs to those who are arriving for Celebration. Behind me are two additional points of greeters with broad smiles welcoming all who come to celebrate. The "leaders" could be huddled in the church kitchen swapping hunting stories and drinking coffee. Instead, we are partnering with God; setting the stage for life transforming experiences.

Let me specifically challenge you to ponder how God may use you in such experiences. Whether you serve as a worship leader, intercessor, pastor, teacher, greeter, parking lot attendant, or cell group leader, God wants to use you to create experiences that touch even the hardest of hearts. What would it look like if you greeted each person at your front door who is coming to the cell gathering with a piping hot cup of coffee or a mug of hot chocolate topped off with marshmallows? As an intercessor, think of the visual experience you are creating by praying through the grounds of your church building or over the chairs in the worship center. As a worship leader, have you ever contemplated taking your guitar (or enlisting a group of bongo players) to the parking lot before the corporate gathering and serenading God with songs of praise?

This "experience" mindset can also be applied to relationships. As I write these words, I am anticipating a visit from a friend whom I have the opportunity to see face-to-face only two or three times a year. I am thinking about the experience that I want to create for our time together. This being the Christmas season, I trust that the outdoor icicle lights and interior decorations that remind us of Christ's birth will enhance our experience this evening. It is a cold night here in Texas and there is nothing like a warm fire in the living room blazing with life as we relax, catch up, and chat. My friend will know that I've taken the time to think about him...to serve him...to display the value that I place on our friendship. I am looking at this evening through the lens of experience.

Pine and Gilmore have made an outstanding deduction which enhances one's understanding and participation in the "experience economy," thus catapulting us to a whole new paradigm of thought. "The second time you experience something, it will be marginally less enjoyable than the first time, the third time less enjoyable than that, and so on until you finally notice the experience doesn't engage you nearly as much as it once did. Welcome to the commoditization of experiences, best exemplified by the increasingly voiced phrase, 'Been there, done that.' "[91]

As I have stated before, I am an avid hunter. Yesterday, I spent some time in the pasture looking for that special whitetail deer. Because I have had this experience numerous times this season, I determined that I longed for an enhanced experience. I determined that I would take out my bow and get close to the action. Sitting motionless for two hours as the deer surrounded my tripod stand proved to be bone chilling—literally. Although I didn't slay a beast of the field, I thoroughly enjoyed my hunting experience. I was up close and personal on the front lines of the action. I learned things that I had never noticed before about the behavior of deer even though I have hunted for nearly two decades. I received fresh wind through the venue of a new experience.

As we look to the "experience economy" for inspiring worship, we acknowledge that it is a multi-layered, evolutionary and continual process that requires prayer, Spirit-led direction, thoughtfulness, and creativity for maximum impact. The maximum impact that we are looking for is not the creation of experiences, but life transformation. We must ask: What set of experiences will bring about the necessary transformation? How can the seeker of Christ (or a life long Christian) be changed from where he is today to where his aspiration lies, or should lie? A transformation, of course, is built on many experiences. "But, no matter how acute an experience, one's memory of it fades over time. Transformations, on the other hand, guide the individual toward realizing some aspiration and then help to sustain that change over time."[92] "While commodities are fungible, goods tangible, services intangible, and experiences memorable, transformations are effectual."[93]

My contention is that life transforming experiences can happen through inspiring worship rooted in passionate spirituality. However, that which sustains such transformations is twofold; our relationship with God, and our relationships with others. This is the message and point of application from the Great Commandment; to love God and others. I have said for many years that messages (preaching) do not ultimately change lives, relationships do. In the next two chapters, I want to share a multitude of stories about people at CCC who have experienced life transformation. You will recognize that the venue for such transformations is one's high regard and continual practice of being in a loving relationship with God and his fellow man.

Let me conclude this chapter with a sobering danger of minimizing the power of life transforming experiences. *Luke 17:11-19* is the gospel account in which Jesus heals ten lepers. You may recall the story. After receiving this healing from the hands of Christ, only one of the lepers returned to Christ *"praising God in a loud voice."* The story teaches us *"he threw himself at Jesus' feet and thanked him—and he was a Samaritan."* Jesus asked this Samaritan leper, *"Were not all ten cleansed? Where are the other nine? Rise and go; your faith has made you well."* An apparent and obvious observation is that nine out of the ten lepers forgot their previous condition. Further, the nine lepers forgot what Christ had done. Yet, one leper returned—the Samaritan leper. Be reminded that during this time there was deep animosity and hatred between the Jews and Samaritans. Religiously, the Samaritans worshiped at Schechem rather than the temple in Jerusalem. Racially, the Samaritans belonged to that mixture of blood that happened between the Assyrians and those who lived in Samaria during the captivity period. Socially, the Jews would not even touch the same drinking vessel as a Samaritan. Additionally, this one Samaritan carried the scourge of leprosy living in desperate and agonizing isolation.

A pertinent question must be asked. Why did the Samaritan leper return to give thanks and praise to Christ? I believe that he was filled with gratitude for Christ's transformation in his life. This attitude of gratitude moved him to worship Christ. Do you know that you will never experience passion in your spiritual life or inspiration in your worship if you are void of gratitude? In other words, gratitude graciously expressed to Christ is the pathway to a passionate walk with Christ and a lifestyle of worship. Without gratitude, you will never worship Christ, our savior and healer. Let us not forget who we are. Let us not forget what Christ has done.

Chapter Nine

"Stories of Love"
(Loving Relationships)

YOU GOTTA DANCE...

The ***Tango*** has the power to pull two strangers together into one, to dance out their desires...to be great lovers and heroes, if only for a moment. This dance is one of glamour in the ballroom filled with passion, allure, and romance. From Paris to Buenos Aires, the *tango* is captivating, enticing, and relentlessly tears down individualism for it takes two to ***tango***!

DANCE WITH ME, DADDY...

Yada [Hebrew]: To revere or worship with extended hands or graceful gestures, to show or point out one's love for another.

*"He [David] appointed some of the Levites to minister before the ark of the Lord, to make petition, **to give thanks, and to praise the Lord**, the God of Israel" (I Chronicles 16:4).*

*"With **praise and thanksgiving** they sang to the Lord: 'He is good; his love to Israel endures forever' " (Ezra 3:11).*

*"Let them **give thanks to the Lord** for his unfailing love and his wonderful deeds for men for he satisfies the thirsty and fills the hungry with good things" (Psalm 107:8-9).*

INTRODUCTION
(by Daren Carpenter, College Network Pastor, CCC)

A person can be completely healthy having great muscle tone and perfect weight. If he has, however, a bad heart, then he is in trouble. So it is with the church body. We can have great buildings, killer worship and incredible speaking, but if the heart is bad then we are in trouble.

1 John 4:12 says *"No one has ever seen God; but if we love one another, God lives in us and his love is made complete in us."* The heart of a healthy church is found in the love that the members have for one another. The healthy heart of the church is seen in the active love displayed from one member to another. I have been on staff in a number of churches in the past, and I have rarely seen the kind of love displayed for each other as I have seen and EXPERIENCED at Cypress Creek Church.

I have seen it in my own life when my fellow pastors

helped furnish my first home. I have seen it when my car was totaled and in a matter of minutes I had students from my cell network on the scene helping gather my belongings and giving me rides. I have seen it as a group of pastors helped build a fence for a fellow team pastor who happens to be a single woman. I have seen it as the church rallied around the members of our youth cell network who were hit with a terrible case of food poisoning at summer camp.

You see, this kind of love is the very heartbeat of a healthy church. I have been so blessed by the relationships of my time here at Cypress Creek Church. To have men who speak truth and correction into my life; to have friends who lend me their vehicles and ears; to have people pray for God to send me a wife (and remind me constantly of their prayers); to be a part of a team that is working together to accomplish a vision bigger than any one of us; these are all manifestations of God's love. No competition, no jealousy, just joy in the journey. Just like the great philosopher DC Talk once said, "Love is a verb." *1 John 3:18* declares; *"Dear children, let us not love with words or tongue but with actions and in truth."* I can not thank God enough for my friends here at CCC and for the love that they show. What a family!

"God loves you." The chances are strong that you have heard the preceding statement thousands of times. Do you wonder what this postmodern generation hears when someone says, "God loves you?" Do they hear "the force lusts after you?" Maybe they hear "God wants something from me and I don't want to give it up." Possibly, this phrase is the catalyst that triggers their defense mechanisms, preparing them for potential hurt and injury. Love is the most important word in any language and also the most confusing. "Love" is used flippantly ("I love.... girls, cars, peanut butter, basketball"). We live in times where love is even used as an excuse for misbehavior. "Well, officer...I beat my wife because she made me mad, but she knows no one loves her more than I do." There is a desperate need to relearn the definition of love.

God is love. Yes, I'll bet you have heard that many, many times in your life as well. Because Jesus is the perfect representation of his Father, he is into love. Jesus is love. Jesus says that love is to be the distinguishing characteristic of his followers. *"A new command I give you: Love one another. As I have loved you, so you must love one another. By this all men will know that you are my disciples, if you love one another" (John 13:34-35).* The Apostle Paul writes, *"Make love your greatest aim" (I Corinthians 14:1, LB).* While on earth, Jesus' love attracted a needy group of friends, wretched tax gatherers, the "unsanctimonious," non-practicing Jewish peasants, and shady outcasts. He was the most loving man who ever lived or who will ever live on this earth.

The sole purpose for a Christian's existence is all about love. *"Love the Lord your God with all your heart and with all your soul and with all your mind. This is the first and greatest commandment" (Matthew 22:37-38).* I don't know about you, but this ultimate call is impossible without God penetrating my life with his love and passion. It is true, therefore, that God is the one who initiates and brings you and me into a love relationship. It is all about him! *"This is how God showed his love among us: He sent his one and only Son into the world that we might live through him. This is love: not that we loved God; but that he loved us and sent his Son as an atoning sacrifice for our sins. We love because He first loved us" (I John 4:9-10, 19).* The prophet Jeremiah reminds us that God *"loves you with an everlasting love"* and has wooed our hearts *"with loving-kindness" (Jeremiah 31:3). Hosea 11:3* expresses the heart of God as he says to us, *"I led them with cords of human kindness, with ties of love; I lifted the yoke from their neck and bent down to feed them."* To be loved by God is the highest relationship, highest feat, and the highest position in life. What you are striving to become will be less than what you already are in Christ.

In Paul's first letter to the needy and troubled church in Corinth, he eloquently explains God's love—His agape to every man. He writes:

Love never gives up. Love cares more for others than for self. Love doesn't want what it doesn't have. Love doesn't strut, doesn't have a swelled head, doesn't force itself on others, isn't always "me first," doesn't fly off the handle, doesn't keep score of the sins of others, doesn't revel when others grovel, takes pleasure in the flowering of truth, puts up with anything, trusts God always, always looks for the best, never looks back, but keeps going to the end. Love never dies (I Corinthians 13:4-8a, The Message).

Apparently, this church was in desperate need of comprehending the specifics of agape—God's highest form of love. Is not the same true for us today? Don't we need agape detailed so that we might have some clue of this great pursuit of life? In Paul's letter to the church in Ephesus, he prays, *"I pray that Christ will live in you as you open the door and invite Him in...and that you will be able to feel and understand, how long, wide, deep, and high His love really is, and to experience this love for yourselves"* (Ephesians 3:16, 19 The Message/LB).

No one tells a story like Jesus. The designation of "master story-teller" falls short of his creativity, expertise, and connectivity. Frequently in the gospels, Jesus speaks of the fine art of shepherding. This was an intricate part of his environment for he was continually around sheep and shepherds. Sheep were dependent on a shepherd to find pasture for them. The task of shepherding entailed finding water, shelter, medication; lending aid in the birthing process; and providing for wounded and weary sheep. Further, Jesus understood the Jewish mind which believed Israel was the flock of God. God was their shepherd and Israel was his flock. In *Luke 15:1-7*, Jesus tells a story couched in this timeless relationship. Before I progress, do you remember who is surrounding Jesus when he shares this story? Yes, the tax collectors and "sinners" were huddled around him. This infuriated the Pharisees and teachers of the law, and they began casting judgment against Jesus for his association with such a desperate lot.

Jesus states, *"Suppose one of you has a hundred sheep and loses one of them. Does he not leave the ninety-nine in the open country and go after the lost sheep until he finds it?"* Notice the condition of a certain member of this flock. This lamb was "lost." Maybe this lamb had moved from one tuft of grass to another and spontaneously worked her little body through a hole in the rock fence. As the shepherd began counting his sheep, he discovered the reality of his flock—one was lost. He would immediately survey the fence striving to find that little hole that enticed the lamb to wander from the flock. The shepherd would "go after" this lost lamb and would not rest "until he finds" her. Jesus adds more punch to this story as he proclaims, *"And when he finds it, he joyfully puts it on his shoulders and goes home."* Allow your mind to embrace this picture. The shepherd finds this little lamb. A broad smile fills his unshaven face. He stoops to pick up this little lamb and notices she is injured. The burly shepherd anoints the cuts and bruises with the gentleness of a mother. Slowly, the lamb is hoisted upon the shepherd's shoulders and she relaxes on the strong muscles of the shepherd's back.

This story is a beautiful picture of God's love for you and me. In our wayward tendencies (and in our lostness), God's searching love ("go after") meshed with the persistence of his grace ("until he finds") is desperately concerned for every single individual—especially those outside the safety and protection of the flock. When any one lamb returns home, there is great rejoicing which illustrates God's response to this recovery mission. God is filled with joy when he finds you!

Because few men individually owned the number of sheep that Jesus cited, the listeners pondered a deeper thought pattern that one could easily overlook in this story. It was quite common for a flock of sheep to be owned communally by a village or a band of shepherds. Couple this thought with the beliefs of those gathered around him—the very flock of God, the people of Israel. Can you now feel the sting of Jesus' words? There are those who are lost yet they consider themselves to be in God's fold. In other words, they don't even know they are lost. Certainly, he is speaking of the Pharisees who are listening to Jesus with no regard for their own lost state. Obviously, they had little sympathy for those who were in that condition. Still, God's love pursues them.

Have you thought about the state of being "lost" recently? A lost person has never felt the love of God, never received his forgiveness, or experienced his indwelling Spirit. Others are lost because they no longer desire the Shepherd to guide their lives. "We'll make it on our own!" is their proud declaration. Some have lost their direction in the multiplicity of alternatives. They have lacked clear conviction of where their lives are headed. Confusion reigns as they fail to consider how each challenge or opportunity fits into a greater plan. Suffice to say that Jesus is interested in "going after" the lost "until he finds," or we find safe pasture in his arms. *"He tends his flock like a shepherd: he gathers the lambs in his arms and carries them close to his heart; he gently leads those that have young" (Isaiah 40:11).*

In case any listener gathered around Jesus might miss his heart of love for the lost, he immediately tells another story. *"Or suppose a woman has ten silver coins and loses one. Does she not light a lamp, sweep the house and search carefully until she finds it?" (Luke 15:8).* Jesus is building on the common knowledge of the people of this time. Everyone listening to this story would know that Jesus is speaking of a woman's frontlet ("semedi") that she would proudly wear signifying her betrothal and marriage relationship to a man. This frontlet symbolized the friendship the woman had with her lover. The loss of one coin from this completed symbol of her lover's gift would alarm the woman to embark on a laborious, extensive and meticulous search (*"search carefully"*) and rescue mission. She would utilize a lamp and a homemade broom to rescue the precious coin. She would not give up *"until"* she discovered the lost coin. Upon the discovery of the lost coin, *"she calls her friends and neighbors together and says, 'Rejoice with me; I have found my lost coin.' " (Luke 15:9).* Can you picture this scene? "Nobody move. I've lost a precious coin from my frontlet. Josiah, be still. Mary, hand me the lamp." The air is permeated with alarm; tension fills the dimly lit room. The eyes of those gathered gaze upon the woman's slow and deliberate motions as she peers into a closet, then under the table. Finally, her trembling hand moves steadily over the dirt floor covered with straw. Dismay grips the hearts of the spectators. Time stands still.

Eventually, the light of the simple lamp reveals a warm glow filling the woman's face. A broad smile ensues, and a collective sigh follows her joyous proclamation, "I found it! I found it! Look, it is here in my hand!" The precious coin rests in her hand's firm grip. Soon, both of her hands are lifted above her head, she grabs her friends, and a spontaneous, celebratory dance commences.

Jesus concludes these two stories by declaring, *"In the same way, I tell you, there is rejoicing in the presence of the angels of God over one sinner who repents" (Luke 15:10).* The lost sheep emphasizes the individualized, caring love of God. Jesus is teaching us the following principle: Possession of the ninety-nine is no substitute for the love of one. The lost coin stresses the personalized concern of God. What's the principle? Jesus' love searches for us, providing completeness when we are found by him. The end result? Yes, joy! All of heaven rejoices over one sinner who turns her heart to God. Assuredly, both stories justify Jesus' welcome of sinners. He is a great lover of the human soul. He created us to love us.

We have seen and heard a double feature, but Jesus doesn't stop there! He continues by telling a story of the perfect Father. I trust you know the story. A father's son prematurely receives his inheritance and leaves for a distant country. His wild living led to the squandering of his riches. Filled with brokenness, he willfully determines to return to his father seeking to be employed as a hired hand. *"But while he [the son] was a long way off, his father saw him and was filled with compassion for him; he ran to his son, threw his arms around him and kissed him" (Luke 15:20).* The son was adorned with a fine robe, a ring was placed on his finger, and sandals were strapped to his feet. A great celebration was at hand as his father exclaimed, *"For this son of mine was dead and is alive again; he was lost and is found" (Luke 15:24).*

As a Texan, I like to picture this reunion in the following manner. On the front porch, Daddy is in the rocking chair scanning the horizon. His eyes move slowly from left to right, right to left, and back again and again. The squeaking rocker appropriately accents the sounds of nature. The sun is dipping, casting its beautiful colors upon the pasture. He sits here every night since his boy left the ranch. Night after night, this was his post-dinner routine. This night, however, is different. In one fluid motion, Daddy leaps to his feet, dismounts the wood planked porch, and runs to the fence line. With great reverence, he removes his Stetson cowboy hat, wipes his sweaty brow with his bandana, and rests his boot upon the lower line of barbed wire. Tears fill his eyes. A slumping figure moves slowly through the dusty ranch road. Daddy sees his boy. He opens his arms and his youngest son vanishes beneath his husky arms. His wayward boy is home!

Pastor Rick Warren shares the following story that will help us to comprehend the agape of a father.

Jenny grew up on a cherry orchard near Travers City, Michigan. Her parents, a little old fashioned, tended to over react to her nose ring, her music and the way she dressed. One night in an argument with her father, she screamed, "I hate you! I never want to see you again!" And that night she ran away, catching a bus to Detroit. The second day in Detroit she met a man with the biggest car she'd ever seen. He offered her a ride, bought her lunch and gave her a place to stay. He even gave her some pills that made her feel better than she'd ever felt in her life. The good life continued for about a year.

That man who she now called "boss" taught her a few things that men liked; and since she was under age, men would pay a premium for her. She lived in a penthouse and ordered room service whenever she wanted. But after a year, she became ill and her boss became mean. Soon, she was out on the streets without a penny to her name. The little bit of money she made turning tricks all went to support her habit. One freezing night on the street sleepless and hungry, Jenny was overwhelmed with a longing to go back home, to the cherry orchards, the warm home and her golden retriever.

Sobbing she called home three times only to get an answering machine. The third time she said, "Mom, Dad, it's me. I want to come home! I'm catching the bus and I'll get there about midnight tomorrow night at the station. If you're not there I guess I'll just stay on the bus to Canada."

On the seven-hour bus trip home Jenny began to have doubts. "What will I say? What will they think? Will they even show up? Will they even be there at the station?" When the bus finally rolled into the small station, the driver announced, "Fifteen minutes, folks! That's all the time we have here. Fifteen minutes!" Fifteen minutes to decide her life. She nervously checked how she looked in a little compact mirror. As she walked into the terminal, nothing could have prepared her for what she saw. Forty people at midnight standing there. Uncles and aunts and cousins and brothers and sisters and mom and dad and grandparents. All of them in silly party hats and blowing silly noisemakers and holding banners and a big banner that stretched the entire terminal that said, "Welcome home!" As her eyes filled with tears, her dad lunged forward out of the crowd to grab her. She said, " Oh, Dad! I am so sorry! I" Her dad said, "Shhhh. We don't have any time for apologies. You're going to be late for the party. We planned a banquet for you at home."[94]

That is a beautiful picture of agape that God has for you. When you come home to God and say, "God, you made me to love me, but I'm disconnected from you. I'm coming home," God throws a party for you. He says, "Welcome home! Welcome into my arms of love." Indeed, God's love is continually wooing you to his heart.

At the beginning of this chapter, I cited the first and greatest commandment (*Matthew 22:37-38*). The second greatest commandment states, *"Love your neighbor as yourself" (Matthew 22:39)*. Please pause where you are as I ask you this question: What is more difficult for you—loving God or loving others?

Take a minute to reflect upon this question. What did you come up with? The large majority of individuals that I have asked this question to respond by saying, "Loving others is the hardest for me! There are so many people that I have trouble loving. God is easy to love. I can't see him with my own eyes and I know he is perfect. It's easy to love someone who is perfect, but more difficult to love those who are imperfect." I certainly concur with this response. Jesus calls us to a great pursuit—loving our neighbor as we love our self!

A few years ago, I was sharing some ministry challenges that I was facing with a fellow pastor, Mike Schlimgen. Methodically, Mike began to teach me the following basic course of life: Loving Relationships 101. I will not soon forget this revelation of "doing relationships" that Mike unfolded for me that day in the town's café nestled close to the banks of the Cypress Creek. God spoke to me through Mike in a profound way. God was saying, "Rob, this is what you've been looking for. Pay attention. Comprehend this and make it a part of your life." As our talk progressed, Mike informed me that he was merely passing along some equipping that he had received from David and Teresa Ferguson (Intimate Life Ministries). In the past few years, God has permeated my heart with his Spirit and allowed this equipping on loving relationships to be a part of my very being. The truths that Mike taught me are embedded deep into my heart, soul, and spirit. This does not mean I am an expert in doing loving relationships! In a nutshell, Mike was used by God to help me know how I might reflect God's love for me to "my neighbor." I have adapted David and Teresa's teaching (found in their book *The Pursuit of Intimacy*[95]) in an effort to "make it my own." Let me share the "four circles of love" with you.

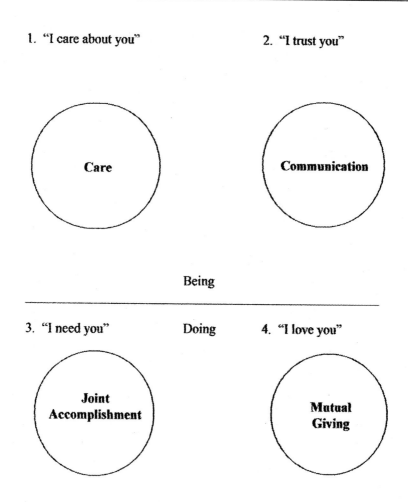

1. "I care about you"

Care

2. "I trust you"

Communication

Being

3. "I need you"   Doing   4. "I love you"

Joint
Accomplishment

Mutual
Giving

The first way I show love to my neighbor is through care. This may be displayed through a word of encouragement, a gentle touch, prayer, listening, and more. I cannot love you if I do not know you. In effect, we model God knowing us for his love letter to us states, *"Lord, you have searched me and you know me" (Psalm 139:1).* God created my inmost being and he knit me together in my mother's womb. I can never hide from God. Further, God knows what every day in my life has been and will be. He knows me totally and completely. Jesus is the perfect representation of his Father and modeled for us this care for others. *"Jesus poured water into the basin and began to wash the disciples' feet" (John 13:5).*

Jesus promises, *"I will come again and receive you to Myself...Peace I leave with you, my peace I give to you...Your sorrow will be turned to joy...Your heart will rejoice and no one takes your joy away" (John 14:3,27; John 16:20, 22).*

The second circle of love is communication. Vulnerable communication with my neighbor says, "I trust you." I will not communicate on a deep level with my neighbor without trust. Our primary way to know God is through his revelation to us. We know God because he tells us about himself. He accomplishes this in a variety of ways including prayer, his Word, and his Holy Spirit. During Jesus' mission on earth, he allowed others to know the Father through vulnerable communication. *"I have called you friends for all things that I have heard from my father I have made known to you" (John 15:15). "From now on you know my father and have seen him" (John 14:7).* Consider the multitude of ways that Jesus communicated God's love for us through the gospels. He desired for us to know God. From the life of Jesus, we can now understand that knowing our neighbor requires communicating our needs, feelings, dreams, fears, thoughts, etc. Please understand that it is one thing for us to know someone, but another thing for someone to know us. Do you know your neighbor? Do your neighbors know you? Build into your life a circle of a few who know you. Communicating with these individuals in an environment of trust will enhance the love in your relationships.

Let's pause and reflect upon these first two circles. First, please note that care and communication are about our "being," not our doing. Most individuals are good at "doing," but infrequently consider their "being." Yet, we were created by God as human "beings," not human "doings." Next, notice that one must pass through care and communication in order to reach mutual giving (or true love). Bypassing these two circles in the pursuit of loving your neighbor can result in heartache, betrayal, and substantial misunderstandings. Finally, let's acknowledge the obvious. Care and communication requires work—real, live vulnerability and transparency with God and our neighbor.

Joint accomplishment is the third circle of love. "I need you" is the permeating voice of this circle. A person who proclaims, "All I need is God" might explore the theological underpinnings of such a statement. We do need God AND we need others. Adam was alone and God provided Eve. Now, consider the following irony and predicament of many individuals: They are doing something with people they don't know and with others who don't care. Now, that's not much of a loving relationship! Wouldn't you agree? Yet, how quickly we run to joint accomplishment without knowing our neighbor. "Let's start a business together...Let's get married...Let's become members of that church." Once again, Jesus models perfectly this process of care, communication and joint accomplishment. *Mark 3:14-15* reads, *"He appointed twelve—designating them apostles— that they might be with him and that he might send them out to preach and to have authority to drive out demons."* Jesus was "with" his disciples. They laughed, played, walked dusty roads, ate, listened, and sang with each other. They involved themselves in the first two circles of love. After being with each other for a period of approximately two years, then Jesus asked his disciples to do something (joint accomplishment). In effect, Jesus invited these twelve ordinary men to participate with him in expanding the kingdom of God's love. Contemplate the following invitations from Jesus to his disciples. *"You also ought to wash one another's feet, for I gave you an example" (John 13:14). "I chose you—that you should go and bear fruit" (John 15:16). "As thou has sent me into the world I also have sent them into the world" (John 17:18). "I am the vine, you are the branches, he who abides in me and I in him, he bears much fruit for apart from me you can do nothing" (John 15:5).* In light of joint accomplishment, we would do well to reflect upon a question recorded in the scriptures which asks, *"Can two walk together, unless they are agreed?" (Amos 3:3).* By walking through care and communication, joint accomplishment has substance, life, and validity.

Finally, we arrive at the fourth circle—mutual giving. "I love you" is this circle's proclamation. As we have already learned, God is love. God says, *"I have loved you with an everlasting love; I have drawn you with loving-kindness" (Jeremiah 31:3).* Jesus said, *"A new commandment I give to you that you love one another even as I have loved you" (John 13:34).* Once again, Jesus helps us to know the Father's love through his modeling. What greater model of love could one be looking for than giving your life for all mankind?

Mutual giving is about dying to our own apathy and selfishness and serving others. Our relationships would be revolutionized if we would roll out of bed each morning looking for ways to serve our neighbor, concurrently dying to our own agenda. Jesus calls us to agape others. Agape love means: "I will live for you," "I will sacrifice for you," "I will care for you," and "I will always speak the truth to you."

Let's not miss the reality of these final two circles. Needing each other to accomplish a certain task (joint accomplishment) and loving each other (mutual giving) are about our "doing." Would you not agree that "doing" is necessary and vital in relationships? They are absolutely vital. Therefore, these four circles of love provide us with a holistic framework for life's relationships. Care and communication ("being") meshed with joint accomplishment and mutual giving ("doing") lead us to fulfilling and life-giving relationships.

As you walk in these four circles of love, please understand that life still happens. Walking and living these circles of love does not mean life will be easy or you will never experience hurt. On the contrary! You will be hurt. You will fail. You will be upset. Others will let you down. In reality, molding your relationships through these four circles of love is an enormous risk. Why? My friend, whenever you choose to love your neighbor and be loved by your neighbor, then you are risking many things. Yet, Jesus took a huge risk on the cross for you and me. Didn't he? There was no guarantee that we would follow him. There was no guarantee that we would recognize and receive his love. There was no guarantee that we would respond to his call and bear fruit. Jesus took a risk with you and me! Will you risk caring for others? Will you risk communicating with your spouse, roommate, children? Will you risk doing things with your neighbor? Will you risk loving others and being loved by others? Most assuredly, love is a risk.

The chapter that follows details for you a multitude of risk takers. They are my fellow risk takers at Cypress Creek Church. Because of God's love, these individuals were able to see outside of themselves and flow in these circles of love. Because of their risks coupled with a love for their neighbors, God has given to us these stories of life.

Chapter Ten

"Stories of Life"
(Holistic Small Groups/Cells)

YOU GOTTA DANCE...

Moshing is an expressive, corporate dance that occurs when bands (usually of the rock, punk and metal genres) play in a live setting. Explaining the essence of the mosh pit without personally seeing it is difficult. At these gigs, members of the crowd will gather at the front and will furiously and passionately shove, push, and body slam each other in time to the music. The idea, however, is not to cause any harm to each other, but just to enjoy the music in an aggressive manner. Unfortunately, personal harm is common. *Moshing* is messy, chaotic (at times), and exhilarating.

It is a fact of life that you will be hurt—whether that be intentional or unintentional. Hurt will come your way. Again, it is a fact of life. Needless to say, life is not a perfectly wrapped package that never comes unraveled. Life can be slipshod and topsy-turvy. The temptation is constant to isolate and alienate yourself when life throws you a curve ball. Don't do it! You will be playing into the enemy's hand. Get into the mosh pit of life—there you will find titanic inspiration.

DANCE WITH ME, DADDY...

Gul, Gil [Hebrew]: To spin around under the influence of any intense emotion including joy, fear, and gladness.

"My enemy will say, 'I have overcome him,' and my foes will rejoice when I fall. But I trust in your unfailing love; my **heart rejoices** *in your salvation. I will sing to the Lord, for he has been good to me" (Psalm 13:4-6).*

"Therefore my **heart is glad***, and my tongue rejoices; my body also will rest secure, because you will not abandon me to the grave. You have made known to me the path of life; you will fill me with joy in your presence, with eternal pleasures at your right hand" (Psalm 16:9-11).*

INTRODUCTION
(by John Church, Youth Network Pastor, CCC)

There is one thing that really motivates me in ministry—changed lives. God has given me the opportunity to stand and watch his Spirit transform the human soul. This has been an exciting, yet humbling experience. Seeing God move a teenager from being lost to leading his/her own cell has changed families, schools, and our church.

Equipping and preparing God's people is a God-given task for any pastor. *"...Some to be pastors and teachers, to prepare God's people for works of service, so that the body of Christ may be built up..." (Ephesians 4:11-12).* The process of preparing a person for leadership is very rewarding but at times very painful. It is the place where God has not only changed teenagers lives but mine as well. Seeing students move from drug addictions, suicide attempts, destructive relationships, to leading a HEART Group has been the most rewarding experience in ministry.

When *one* student decides to follow Jesus with his life, people are watching. Their families, friends, teachers, and coaches are all watching. It changes whole communities when it happens over and over. It starts with preparing a person to live and lead for God.

Seeing students equipped for cell leadership, baptizing cell members, teaching, and ministering to the needs of their friends has changed hundreds of lives over the past few years. Every year gets more exciting as spiritual momentum is built across our region. What a privilege it has been to work with such a great team and serve the youth of Wimberley and beyond.

The "stories of life" that follow are just a few experiences that validate and affirm his dancing hand in our midst. These stories were penned by CCC members who desire to share their story with you.

"...I was a stranger and you invited me in." Matthew 25:35

My husband and I began attending Cypress Creek Church in November 1999. We had just received news that I was pregnant with our first child. We knew no one in Wimberley. We took a chance attending CCC after a distant relative suggested this sort of church. We were a little worried when we approached the worship center so we looked around for a while before we finally gave in to checking it out. When we finally did, it was an instantaneous and mutual response of exhilaration! This was exactly the kind of church we were looking for. We immediately met eight to ten people who introduced themselves to us. One lady my age invited us to HEART group (cell). The group members took us in like little babes; loving us, listening to us, and accepting us. Even though they had no clue who we were, what we believed, or where we were from. It didn't matter to them. In HEART group they extended sincere and genuine care for us.

Honestly, for a while I couldn't understand why someone would be so nice and take such great efforts to serve us. The one lady who initially invited us to HEART group was constantly calling, sending notes, and even gave me most of the things from her nursery for our baby (who was yet to be born). No one had shown so much care, not even people from our own families. It's easy to give to people you know, but to give to people you don't know, without expecting anything in return says a lot! After we had our daughter, we were told we would have meals brought to our home every night for two weeks. It brought tears to my eyes knowing these people thought enough of us to take time out of their own lives to serve. Having our baby was such an exhausting experience. It was a time when I really needed to feel supported, cared for, and important. Why would these strangers do something so nice? Either they were weird, just born nice, or they were doing it for some specific reason. What I couldn't understand then, but do now, is that they were doing it out of obedience to God's command to serve others. Still, it was more than that. They served with such joy and happiness. They served us gladly and it made such an imprint on my life. They didn't treat us like we were a burden to them. Instead, it was an honor for these people to be used by God to serve us.

Please understand, when we began going to CCC we were both believers, but I had strayed from the Lord and had made some big mistakes as a result of my disobedience and rebellion. I could not believe God would take me back. I thought I would just work real hard and maybe I could somehow get God to like me again—especially if I punished myself long enough. Through these expressions of kindness, selflessness, genuine concern, care, love, support, and nurture, I have been able to get back into God's family and under his umbrella of protection. Through the ministry of this church body, I have learned that you can't work to receive God's love and acceptance. He has already accepted me, loves me, and most of all, He adopted me. He knew I wouldn't be faithful, but He never let go. The people in my HEART group didn't know where I'd been, but they did know that God accepted me, therefore they accepted me. It was the grace of God demonstrated through their love that taught me to accept God's love for me. Now I am able, because of God's grace and strength, to reciprocate this same kind of love to others. It motivates me to please God and love others—now that I know how much I am loved. Through Christ, cell life helped start this new beginning, this fresh start, and this regeneration of my spiritual being. Thanks to my God and Savior, Jesus Christ!

"Great is the Lord, and most worthy of praise...." Psalm 48:1

I spent most of my adult life as a functioning drunk. Out of desperation, I finally sought help from Alcoholics Anonymous where the solution to alcohol abuse is living a God-dependent life. I have found over the years that coming to God for help with any problem is the right and correct path to trod. At this time, however, I still had little use for religion and Christ, continuing to place that blame upon my childhood church experiences and a television evangelist. In hindsight, I was just seeing what I wanted to see.

My wife and son had attended church, mostly without me, for some years by the time we moved to the Wimberley in 1999. I think out of guilt, I went searching for a new church for THEM when we came upon Cypress Creek Church. Surprisingly, we knew the greeter (turns out he knows everyone) and a few other members of the church. Additionally, I was really attracted to the music. I filled out the welcome card one Sunday morning during Celebration and was shocked when Pastor Eddie (the Worship leader) called and wanted to meet. Sneaky CCC, they sent the guy to whom I could probably most relate.

Even through my wall of resistance, Eddie had a way of reaching me. He never chastised my doubts or questions, or me for having them. In fact, he encouraged them. By the time he suggested the family attend a HEART group, I was at least willing to try this one time though I didn't really want to. I had no idea how much I would eventually grow to love these people, or just how much they would mean to my family and me in the months to come. Eddie also got me involved in the worship ministry of the church. At first, I resisted, but now it offers incredible spiritual growth and experience. I slowly figured out that if Eddie suggested something and I felt resistance, then I should go ahead and do it anyway. In spite of all my efforts to not belong, one Saturday morning I found myself opening the church building to prepare for a HEART group that my wife and I would facilitate (yes, this was Eddie's suggestion). I remember feeling stunned that I actually was part of a church and loved it!

In the fall of 2001, I was diagnosed with cancer. Immediately prayers began within our original HEART group and spread throughout CCC (it is a POWERFUL experience to have folks sincerely praying over you) and other friends and family. My wonderful earthly surgeon found a bit more cancer than expected necessitating probable radiation and chemotherapy treatments. During this time my family and I were inundated with prayers AND meal after meal, good deed after good deed, much of which was orchestrated by our cell members. Prayer and action, what a wonderful combination.

Radiation was devastating. However, as CCC continued to emphasize God's ENORMOUS love for me and MY need to let GOD'S will work through my life, I felt little fear during this time knowing God was positioning me to best serve Him. He had this cancer and the prognosis right where He wanted it. After the impact of radiation, my oncologist offered a somewhat unusual suggestion of waiting before preceding with chemotherapy. Long story short, some seven months after surgery I still show not a trace of cancer and have another two months before even testing for cancer again. The cancer has been such a blessing. The amount of love my family and I have received has been astounding. God has again equipped me, as with my alcoholism, to be of service to others (as was done for me by other CCC members) with cancer as only one who has experienced it can. And what a great reminder for me to fully experience and value each precious day, person, and event here on earth.

I continue trying daily, with varying success, to allow God's will for me to work in my life. When I surrender to this, I find the fears and anxieties of life are replaced with peace and serenity. The lasting kind offered only by our loving Father.

"Give, and it will be given to you. A good measure, pressed down, shaken together and running over, will be poured into your lap. For with the measure you use, it will be measured to you."

Luke 6:38

My family and I have been with Cypress Creek Church from day one. Now there has been much more gained for the church body other than numbers, but those numbers do tell a story—HIS-STORY. We have been rock solid in church for the past eighteen years, not counting childhood. For the first nine years (1984 to 1992), my family and I were in a radical church filled with religion, rules and rituals. While it overall was good and needed, we suffered dearly financially. Prosperity was taught, but not stewardship. I named and claimed and blabbed and grabbed, but grew further in the hole. I mean big time in the hole! In 1990 (and at the end of my rope), I cried out to the Lord and He heard me and led me to another radical change in regard to our finances. My income that year increased 95%. This was the beginning of our walk in the way of a steward. God then started preparing us for a move, a move to CCC. This was when CCC was initially "inside" of Pastor Rob, starting to form and grow. We called him when we heard of what was about to happen and we knew that we were to hook our wagon to this move of God.

From 1984 to 1992 our total gross income was $315,000. That is a combined GROSS average of $35,000 per year. We started with CCC and received Biblical counseling. We took in everything CCC had to offer in order to better ourselves. We were in another radical church, but the main thing was and still is relationships, responsibility, and rewards. One on One Discipleship with our cell members, experiencing our freedom in Christ, learning that our significance is hinged to the cross of Christ, and many other practical and useable teachings from our leaders have yielded many, many rewards for us. I personally had come from a place where my acceptance and security were wrapped up in my position in and at the church. Over this past nine years, God through CCC has walked me out of that to where my security is in Him and what He says and thinks about me—period. Learning and living the Christian walk of faith based on relationship vs. religion is the truth, the way and the life. It is all about our relationship with Christ that starts this flow.

The last nine years have yielded many positive personal, family and financial changes as well. We have eliminated thousands and thousands of dollars of debts. We wholeheartedly believe the fact *that because we were faithful tithers alone, God closed the deal on one debt that was over $50,000. I have my prayer list from One on One Discipleship where a multitude of prayers were answered right down the line. We have seen ONLY increase in EVERY area of our lives. I have even added a few pounds. God has been so faithful and continues to grant us the desires of our hearts. Stewardship works and we are living proof. One of our Overseers said to me once, "If you work the principles, then they will work for you." We knew about them, but having them taught and modeled to us has been of great value. In the past nine years, our total gross income has tripled. We did not try to make this happen, we just did what we were taught and God did the rest. We have even goofed up from time to time. I try not to even think about it. I just remember my written life purpose that Pastor Rob taught me to write and get to work. All of this may go away tomorrow, but what has happened has made HIS-STORY. HIS story in us and through us has been great.*

"I will repay you for the years the locusts have eaten..."
Joel 2:25

God kept nudging me at the beauty shop to reach out to a pitiful young woman who had recently come to work there. Her name was Shirley and she drove a beat up car, had a troubled and troublesome little child, and lived with an abusive man. After I had ignored God for several weeks I finally asked her if she would do One on One Discipleship with me. I will never forget the alacrity with which she said, "Yes." We met on the back terrace at the beauty shop when she had an hour free.

God's work in and through Shirley has been amazing. She is a dear friend to me today. Currently, she leads a HEART group. I love this woman. She has endured much, but she is more than a conqueror through God's power and Spirit. She is a fighter, and has developed maturity, and loves the Lord and understands CCC's vision. Her strength and clear thinking are amazing, and the transformation of her child is also amazing.

"Ask and it will be given to you; seek and you will find; knock and the door will be opened to you. For everyone who asks receives; he who seeks finds; and to him who knocks, the door will be opened."   *Matthew 7:7-8*

I remember the first time we journeyed to a CCC HEART group. I remember being so thrilled to sit in a living room and talk about the Lord with a group of people and worship the Lord in such a sweet environment. As a big fan of C.S. Lewis, I have always longed to sit and visit with him, sipping on tea and discussing deep "Lewis spiritual ideas." Well, Lewis was not in that living room, but the sweet fellowship was addicting. We were hooked.

As I think back and reflect upon God's activity in our midst, I remember the many prayers that God so faithfully answered. Distinctively, I remember the thrill of being in the presence of someone coming to the Lord for the first time. It is like seeing a baby being born, but without the horrible mess! I remember when a dear friend was newly divorced and struggling just to make it through another day. She went to the doctor to discover a lump in her breast (her mother was a survivor of breast cancer). She came to HEART group the Sunday before she was to go to a surgeon for a final sonogram. We laid hands on her and PRAYED—warfare kind of praying—and you can guess the outcome! She went to the doctor and the tumor was completely gone! This experience was definitely a faith builder for everyone in our cell. This miracle increased our intimacy with God and each other. Many times in HEART group, ministry would come simply from a kind word or a warm hug. Now that I think about it, I have lots of stories of the many amazing things that God has done in our midst. Cell life is not complicated. It is really quite simple. When people connect in a cell, pray and care for one another, it is as if the power of the Lord is released. All we need to do is participate with God who is in our midst and ready to work.

"He has sent me to bind up the brokenhearted, to proclaim freedom for the captives and release from darkness for the prisoners,...They will rebuild the ancient ruins and restore the places

long devastated,...They will be called oaks of righteousness, a planting of the Lord for the display of his splendor." **Isaiah 61**

Our story with Cypress Creek Church began in 1999. I must go back some to help this story make sense. My husband, Johnny and I were married right out of high school at the ripe old ages of eighteen and nineteen. Johnny and I did not come from Christian homes. We both came from divorced homes. You could say we had not been shown how to maintain loving relationships. In 1998, after having two children, we could not seem to get along. We were both in search of something to fill the void that only God could fill. For us, we followed what we knew best and separated. It was during this time that God's Holy Spirit found us. We were very low and hungry for an answer. I like to say this is where the love affair began; a love affair, that is, with Jesus Christ.

This love relationship started with small steps and has grown to a deep personal connection that we could no longer live without. On Easter Sunday of 1999, I was invited to a CCC Celebration by a church member. Her persistence was amazing. I figured if I went she would stop asking me to go, but I had no clue what I was in for. That Sunday, I heard of a Savior who endured unexplainable pain and suffering for the world, and for me. He had suffered for me— sinful, filthy, ungrateful me. During this message, I was told that Jesus would come to where I was and minister to my heart, because he loved me. I received a new understanding of what the cross of Jesus really meant. I fell in love, and God put a hunger for more as I received Jesus as my personal Lord and Savior.

Immediately, I began telling Johnny about church and how the people were so real and humble. After a few months, he came with me to church, and God began doing a great work in his heart. We had been sitting behind a couple and their children at church for a few weeks, and they invited us to their HEART group. We were told that these were weekly gatherings in homes throughout the county that allowed people to build relationships with each other. We soon discovered why Pastor Rob repeatedly stated, "HEART groups are the heart beat of CCC." I started going to the group and it was so awesome. After the first meeting, even though I knew no one, I felt *like I was right at home.*

Throughout the years, we continued meeting with this cell and built very strong connections with these people. We all cried together, laughed, and shared intimate details of the works that Jesus was doing in our lives. Johnny and I also participated in a "Marriage Enrichment" course that helped us through the hurdles in our marriage. We truly received so much from it, and by God's grace we can now live out the principles we learned. Further, the women of our HEART group participated in an Encounter weekend retreat. During this time, we gave up many strongholds and prayed intensely for one another. We took the next step of intimacy with God by trusting Him with our sins and being set free from our sins. We had prayer partners and God put me with a woman who would become a wonderful friend to me. God is good! God had big plans for the relationship he was building between us.

As time went on, Johnny and I became very close to my friend and her husband. We would journey to HEART group consistently with this couple. We even lived with them for a while because of some circumstances that came our way. It was definitely God's work because we had four children and four adults living under one roof, and there was never even a squabble or hurt feelings. One week our HEART group shepherd asked us to speak at Celebration about the power of HEART groups. That Saturday night before the Sunday Celebration, both Johnny and my friend's husband had Holy Spirit revelations. They were awakened during the night and given a word from God! God told them to multiply out of our home HEART group and begin a HEART group focusing on reaching the lost and equipping leaders.

It was not long after this experience at Celebration that the enemy tried to discourage us. Johnny had a serious accident and was hospitalized. "The thief comes only to steal and kill and destroy: I have come so that they may have life, and have it to the full" (John 10:10). There was no chance for discouragement. Our HEART group and church body carried us through this trying time. Johnny and I were overwhelmed with joy at the love we were shown. We soon got our new HEART group under way and God brought us people to shepherd. We realized the more prayer *invested in a cell, the more fruit we would see. God began to speak to Johnny and me about expanding our ministry. We were able to go on a ministry trip to Mexico where we felt God pulling on our hearts. God rarely reveals the full vision to his disciples all at once, but when we walk in line with His will it cultivates faith and wonderful things happen. During this ministry trip with our fellow CCC members, we grew very close to all of them.*

CCC had been planning to multiply out a team to plant a new church to further God's kingdom. A few months after the trip, the pastor we had gone with to Mexico (Pastor Eddie) was called by God to be the pastor of the new church. When this was announced one Sunday at Celebration, Johnny and I knew we were being called to multiply out of our HEART group and to help plant this new church. This new church has a deep focus on missions and bringing into the church non-believers. With great joy coupled with the desire to serve God, we multiplied out of CCC and are a part of a well equipped church planting team. There has been intense prayer surrounding the planting of this church and we expect God to build an awesome fellowship. Cypress Creek Church's vision statement is "Building a Community, Changing a City, Reaching a Country [and world]." We have truly seen in countless ways that vision unfold. As the body of Christ, we have learned to encourage one another, equip leaders, and serve fellow communities and nations. The love story does not end here. We have just begun our journey's walk with a Holy God. What we have been given by God's grace, I pray, will last for generations to come.

"All the believers were together and had everything in common...They gave to anyone as he had need." Acts 2:44-45

Michaela and family (three girls—two young children and one newly born infant) moved in with us last September. Dan (husband and father) is working overseas and the plan is for the family to join him soon. However, at the time, Michaela was pregnant with their third child and wanted to stay here until the birth. They have shipped all their household belongings overseas including their Honda minivan. Dan's plan was that Michaela and the girls would drive the red 1986 Ford F150 truck with a 351 V-8 carbureted engine. To make sure the truck was in tiptop shape for his bride and two (soon to be three) daughters (all in carseats), Dan replaced the carburetor before he left in September.

Everything was going splendid until the truck started stalling on Michaela. I looked at it and discovered that the carburetor was leaking gas. I tried to make some temporary repairs to hold it over until Dan came back, which he did when the baby was born in late December. While he was here, Dan took the new carburetor back to the auto supply store and exchanged it. This second "new" carburetor had immediate problems, and just before he had to leave again, Dan took this one back to exchange it for a third "new" carburetor. This third one didn't leak, but it idled so low that the truck would die at every stop. But, Dan had to fly back to his assignment overseas and we decided that I would drive the truck and loan Michaela my car.

Last Monday, I struggled with the truck—left foot on the brake, right foot on the gas to keep it running, sliding the gearshift into neutral so I wouldn't accidentally spurt thru an intersection ... very tricky, very dangerous. On Tuesday morning, I drove the truck to Pastor Jim's house for our cell network team meeting. Since I was the first one there, I popped the hood and decided to tinker with the idle adjustment. That didn't work, so I tried adjusting the float valve in the first chamber of the carburetor. Unfortunately, the float valve popped out and I could not get it back in. Apparently, the drillings for the threads were stripped! I had to leave the truck at Jim's house.

My wife took me to work that day, and my colleague, who works for me, gave me rides for the next few days. I was trying to figure out how to solve the truck problem, and the thought came to me "Just have that truck towed to the town's mechanic." Within a minute, the phone at the office rang, and it was Pastor Jim. He said that he'd been thinking about the truck, and why didn't I just have it towed over to the town's mechanic and let him fix it! So, that's what we did. I called the mechanic, and explained the problem, trying to help him understand that it wasn't my truck, or my wife's truck—but that I was driving it and would he repair it? He agreed. The truck *was repaired for minimal expense.*

Now, let's look at this! Dan, Michaela, Pastor Jim, my colleague, the mechanic, my wife and I were involved in this somewhat irritating fiasco. But God touched our lives with his powerful love through this frustrating carburetor! We experienced this church body pull together as a family reflecting his love with the potential of touching one not-yet-believer—the mechanic! It's a joy to be part of his family, watching his love flow to his children!

"As you have seen me do, so do likewise." Luke 10:37

My experience with Cypress Creek Church has allowed me the opportunity to be involved with many different walks of life. Before I became a member of CCC, my relationships were limited to the people I worshiped with. As I think back, I realize how narrow my scope was and how ineffective I was for Christ. However, when we became part of a church dedicated to reaching the unchurched, I didn't realize how many different people there are out there. It definitely took me out of my comfort zone and required me to interact with people on a whole different level.

Examples that come to my mind include intervening when a cell member's husband was threatening suicide, moving a young woman that the cell was seeking to help out of an abusive home, and opening our home to a troubled teen. I was not equipped for any of these experiences, but I found that if I would stay obedient to God, he would equip me for the unexpected. These were messy and definitely stretching experiences. Often when I felt confused and frustrated about circumstances, I would run to Pastor Rob and ask him how to minister, why this was happening, etc. He would always encourage me, but mostly he would shrug his shoulders and point me back to the cross. I realized then that he didn't have all the answers and didn't want to be the one with all the answers. He pointed me to the One that did.

Currently, I am in unchartered waters once again in my life. I direct a ministry for women who are experiencing unexpected pregnancies. Often we have the privilege to witness to them about the love of Jesus Christ and rejoice with them when they receive Jesus

Christ as their Savior. We then get them plugged into a local church and continue a relationship with them throughout their pregnancy. We are able to extend hope and forgiveness to a woman that has experienced an abortion in her past and is experiencing guilt, fear, and grief. What a joy it is to see her freed from the bondage of past sin and begin to walk in freedom and new life! We also are able to extend accountability and encourage sexual purity to those that seek our services. Certainly, I do see all walks of life, but now I am able to see that they are just people the same as me who desperately need God in their life.

"Be joyful always; pray continually; give thanks in all circumstances, for this is God's will for you in Christ Jesus."
I Thessalonians 5:16-18

For the last four years, I have made nineteen visits to the hospital and numerous trips to Austin for my chemotherapy treatments. Today, I received word from my doctor that as of now I am cancer free!! Praise God for his fantastic blessings.

There is no question in my mind but that this miracle is an act of God because of His tremendous love for me. His healing was done in His timing—not mine. Please don't think I'm too weird, but God loves me so much that He shared this healing with me in a dream this past Saturday night—two days before I received the official call. In this dream, my doctor walked up to me where I was sitting and sat down beside me on the bench. He placed his right arm around me and with a huge smile on his face, he told me that I was cancer free.

I'm also convinced that this act of God was a result of the thousands of prayers from all over the world that have been said on my behalf. Prayers from Korea, Japan, South America, Mexico, Cuba, children in schools where I used to teach, and especially the powerful, fervent and consistent prayers from Cypress Creek Church. I'm not sure I understand all that has happened to me these past few months, but it began last summer when I caught the vision God has for me.

In recent months, I have been delivered from strongholds such *as anger, resentment, and many others. I understand the value of knowing the truth, being totally honest, and being obedient to our Lord and Savior Jesus Christ. These things simply would not have occurred had it not been for Cypress Creek Church. Now, I finally understand why we searched and found CCC nine years ago. Glory to God, and "it's" only the beginning.*

The "Body of Christ" has a whole new meaning to me now, and I truly do understand when one part of the body suffers, the whole body suffers. I knew how to handle "living" with cancer, now I have to learn how to live without cancer; it'll be fun learning.

"I waited patiently for the Lord; he turned to me and heard my cry. He lifted me out of the slimy pit, out of the mud and mire; he set my feet on a rock and gave me a firm place to stand. He put a new song in my mouth, a hymn of praise to our God..."
Psalm 40:1-3a

In 1993, Pastor Rob received a vision to plant Cypress Creek Church. I learned of this adventure through various people in the community. Rob seemed so young...of course, I had forty years on him (and I still do!). At the time, I was a dumb sheep. I knew the Great Shepherd, but had no meaningful relationship with him. Like a sheep, I was hungry, searching, looking for food—which I assumed was to be found in the church. I was being fed by a dear friend who was serving at a local church, but he eventually moved on.

My wife and I were intrigued with CCC—a cell church without a building, committees, or covered dish suppers. The church seemed to be designed so that one would have time for job, family, and other pursuits, but at the same time—pursue God through a cell (a set of relationships) and Celebration (corporate worship). The church, therefore, would not be worshiped, but God. We would have time for our lives, especially time to pray and worship our Lord.

As CCC got started in a renovated feed store, I sat in the back so I might come in late after the worship music during Celebration, hear a good sermon, and slip out early. On a certain Sunday morning, the entry door to the worship center squeaked, and I tried to help by not letting this physical irritation disturb the message.

Since I was by the door, I was asked to hand out "opportunity folders" (bulletins) each Sunday. Therefore, Sunday after Sunday I would arrive early to perform this service. When the second Celebration service started, I stayed for that too, for some reason. In so doing, I got to hear both hours of the contemporary, up-beat music which to me was unfamiliar, repetitious, long, not worshipful, and loud! I just knew I was correct in my evaluation of the music—and I was wrong! I began observing that the worship attracted the young people to church—lots of them! Seeing and hearing of the many miracles which were happening made it evident that the worship was changing lives—including mine.

It was said that people came to CCC for three reasons: worship, teaching, and relationships. When I realized that the worship music we experienced was Biblical, Spirit-filled, enthusiastically presented, not to mention effective, I succumbed too. The messages presented by Pastor Rob and our other pastors were carried home with me. They were informative and enlightening. For a while, I just knew Rob's messages were presented just for me. So timely! I was learning, being fed at last.

Further, I learned a vast amount concerning relationships. I found it easy to love the loveable and avoid the rest. To love those who were irresponsible, in debt, with marriage problems, sick, on drugs, self-centered, and dishonest was another story. The cell I attended was filled with such folks. "They have so much to learn," I thought smugly. But, then I realized I had even more to learn than they did! I was not living a life that Jesus would desire for me. So the result might be said to be the renewing to a life of a seventy-year-old man with more love, compassion, forgiveness, faith, and prayer in seeking a better relationship with all—especially our Lord Jesus Christ.

"I, the Lord, have called you in righteousness; I will take hold of your hand. I will keep you and will make you to be a covenant for the people and a light for the Gentiles, to open eyes that are blind, to free captives from prison and to release from the dungeon those who sit in darkness." **Isaiah 42:6-7**

At the age of thirty-eight, I went to federal prison in Louisberg, Pennsylvania. The legal authorities told me I would spend six months behind bars. I was mixed up with the wrong people, taking business money I made and pushing drugs from New York City to Maine. For four years in various prisons throughout the country, I learned a whole new way of life.

One night, I went up to the prison chapel and thought about all the Christians in my life that tried to help me, including my mom and dad. I began to feel broken on the inside. Here I was in prison, having everything stripped away from me including my children, freedom, and more. Bending to my knees, I cried out to Jesus and said, "This has to change. Enough is enough!" I asked Jesus Christ to come into my heart. I desired to be like some of the Christian friends I knew that had a life and a purpose. I said to Jesus, "Please do not let me out of prison until my feet are on solid ground. I will never leave you, Lord. We will always be together." This is when and where I began my relationship with Jesus Christ.

After spending one year in this prison in Pennsylvania, I was expedited to a Huntsville, Texas penitentiary. I was moved around to twenty-nine different States and thirty-three different prisons. At one time, I spent ten days on a prison chain gang. At each stop in my journey, I would pray that God would provide me an opportunity to study the Bible with other prisoners and be a part of a prison church. Eventually, I was assigned to the Holiday Unit in Texas which was known as "God's School for Prisoners."

Upon arrival at the Holiday Unit, I walked into the prison's gymnasium that was transformed into a church gathering. Four hundred men were lifting their hands to God, praising God in a vibrant, collective song of worship. God's presence was thick and real. For the next thirty-three months, I worshiped in this prison church. My prayers were answered!

My parole hearing was fast approaching and I continually prayed to God. "God, if I am released, please allow me to find a church where Jesus is present." God placed a peace in my heart and said to me, "I have a place for you." My parole was official and I was released to Wimberley, Texas where my sister and her family resided.

My first Sunday in Wimberley, my sister and brother-in-law brought me to Cypress Creek Church. At that time, CCC was worshiping in the Jr. High gymnasium. I couldn't believe my eyes. As we entered the gymnasium, there I saw 350 people standing and worshiping God. I looked around the gymnasium and glanced at the basketball goals. God took me back to my prison church in the Holiday Unit. God is good!! At this worship service, God showed me my wife to be. In a few years, I married this beautiful woman. The list goes on and on concerning God's goodness to me and my family. As the years unfolded, God allowed my family to be a part of a church planting team in a nearby town.

Thank you, God, for your patience with me. Thank you for your perfect timing. My life is very different now and this could have never transpired without my loving friends at CCC. They embraced me despite my past. They loved me despite my immaturity. They challenged me to be all that I could be for the cause of Christ.

Chapter Eleven

"Smoldering Ashes and Dancing Fires"
(Gift Oriented Ministry)

YOU GOTTA DANCE...

The ***Swing***, the ***Shag***, the ***Jitter Bug*** and the ***Jive*** are dances in the same family that share similar patterns including rapid under arm turns and spinning. The style and tempo, however, are the distinguishing differences among these dances. The music is diverse, from 50s Rock and Roll, Big Band, Rhythm and Blues, and a variety of today's music. The ***Shag*** originated in Myrtle Beach, South Carolina, and is typically a dance exhibiting fancy footwork with very little upper body movement, compared to its sister dances. Beach music and blues is the choice for ***shaggers***. The ***Swing*** is the most versatile of these dances. With a wide range of music to choose from one can swing to almost anything. The ***Jive*** is the fastest and is often called the "single time swing." Looking to get your heart rate excited? If so, then try the ***Jive***—a dance filled with acrobatic moves and lifts which are also found in the ***Jitter Bug***, another fast dance.

You may *jive* or you may *swing*. Some of you can *jitter bug* with the best of them. And then there are others who simply *shag*. Indeed, there are different dances within the same family. Whatever dance you dance, know that you have a gift. Utilize your gift to electrify the body...and the party!

DANCE WITH ME, DADDY...

Chagag [Hebrew]: To move in a circle, to march in a sacred procession, to celebrate with leaping, to reel to and fro.

*"These things I remember as I pour out my soul: how I used to go with the multitude, **leading the procession** to the house of God, with **shouts of joy and thanksgiving** among the festive throng" (Psalm 42:4).*

INTRODUCTION
(by Kathryn Duffie, Inter-generational Network Pastor, CCC)

"The priesthood of all believers?" That was just a phrase I could not grasp during my forty-two years in the traditional church. I saw leaders and a few others doing all the tasks; many just sitting in the pews on Sundays. I poured out my frustration to a wise man one time and his answer was firm. "Don't you know that Jesus tells us that His yoke is easy and His burden is light?" he asked. That changed how I chose acts of service, but only now do I know the reality of that scripture.

In service at Cypress Creek Church, I have been trained for my tasks and have learned that my tasks use my God-given gifts. From the beginning, we have had some form of a track for training leaders, those people who grasped the vision and were willing to grow. Also we have used various ways to help people identify their gifts and their role in His kingdom.

As I pastor my team and help them pastor their teams, I utilize my God given, grace gifts. I am content and joyful in my role and know that I function "less in my own strength and more in the power of the Holy Spirit." My yoke is easy and my burden is light.

In the previous chapter, you were bombarded with stories displaying God's dancing (and loving) hand through various sets of relationships (cells). An astute reader recognized the undergirding grace gifts that radiated through these cells such as mercy, helps, hospitality, discernment, evangelism, leadership, worship, teaching and more. As God created the human body to survive and prosper by providing oxygen, food, and water, he further created the spiritual body (the body of Christ) to survive and prosper through the release of gifts which flow into the body's cells through the Holy Spirit. When God grants and releases his gifts, he grants and releases himself. Gifts cannot be discounted as "things." His gifts are a manifestation of himself. When the gifts are present and operative, he is present and operative.

A few years ago, I taught a message at CCC's Celebration entitled, "Smoldering Ashes and Dancing Fires." The teaching centered on the Holy Spirit and spiritual gifts and the title was rooted in a youthful scenario in my life. As a Jr. High student, my friend (Mark) and I were packing up our belongings after a weekend retreat with other young people from our church. As I checked the cabin for any stray personal articles, I heard a deafening cry. It was Mark who was running like a madman to the land behind the cabin and screaming, "Fire! Fire!" I didn't pay much attention at first because Mark was quite a prankster. And then I thought to myself, "Could those ashes from the cabin's fireplace I placed in the tall grass behind the cabin have caused a fire?" For the sake of security, I moved to the back window of the cabin and peered out only to see Mark attacking a dancing fire with his black wool sailor's coat. I was guilty. Just minutes earlier, I had taken the ashes (which in my uneducated estimation were fully extinguished) and displaced them in the field behind our cabin. Needless to say, Mark and I didn't catch the first bus back to civilization. Our youth pastor assigned us to a new task— making sure the smoldering ashes were totally and completely doused before boarding any bus to freedom. To this day, I have a "burning" mental image of Mark (with great determination etched on his face) awkwardly running with his lanky body in full motion rushing to the fire. He left the encampment as a hero—I was the goat.

I know in my knower that there are smoldering ashes ready to catch the wind of the Spirit creating a dancing fire in hundreds of churches around the globe. At the camp in my younger days, the dancing fire was not a good thing, but consider *Luke 3:16: "He [Christ] will baptize you with the Holy Spirit and with fire."* This baptism by fire (the "dancing fire") is a good thing symbolizing God's consuming, purifying power in the life of a believer. I know that there are tiny sparks of gifted people in the body of Christ ready to be a part of this dancing fire of God. Yet, these individuals are merely smoldering ashes who have been squelched and sometimes snuffed out. As one pastor told me several years ago, "Rob, be careful with those spiritual gift type churches. Things can get crazy real quick if you don't watch it." Figuratively and symbolically, this pastor was beating down a dancing fire in my heart. He was not "into" God's people ministering in the church through their God-given gifts. He desired control, order, and "the call" on how God would move.

Over two hundred years ago, one of the founding fathers of this nation, Benjamin Rush, had a dream. In this dream, a man was climbing atop Christ's Cathedral Church in Philadelphia and began turning the weather vane. In effect, he had reversed the relationship between the weather vane and the wind. As Mr. Rush awakened, he analyzed this dream. He concluded that the weather vane upon the majestic church building was not a manipulator of the wind, but simply an indicator of which direction the wind is blowing. As he pondered the dream, he sensed he was the man ascending the church's roof. In his critical role during the founding of our nation, he was convicted of trying to change the events of the time rather than indicate them. *"The wind blows wherever it pleases. You hear its sound, but you cannot tell where it comes from or where it is going. So it is with everyone born of the Spirit" (John 3:8).* Are you a manipulator or an indicator of God's activity in your midst? Trying to manipulate the Spirit of God is not new news. One simply needs to read the books of *Acts* to see such behavior.

In the early church, no person is more poignantly present than the Holy Spirit. The decisions and directions of men and women were rooted in the moving of the Holy Spirit. Despite this reality, their were missteps, mistakes, misjudgments—you know, sin. The following three snapshots from the *Acts* of the apostles through the Holy Spirit should serve as cautions for us in this realm of manipulation.

First, we may attempt to manipulate the Holy Spirit through organization (*see Acts 1:15-26).* Although God told the disciples to wait, Peter wanted to organize. His organization was filled with biblical interpretation (*v. 20*), appropriate nominations *(v. 23),* and election (*v. 26*). The organization was impressive—it looked good, but it contained no dynamic of God. Have you noticed another mention of the elected disciple named Matthias anywhere else in scripture? Please understand that I am not proposing through this scenario that the Holy Spirit is the sponsor of disorganization. We must submit the organization to God, not God to the organization. Here is the principle I want you to take hold of: The church should be so full of life that people beg for structure rather than the church being so full of structure that the people beg for life.

Second, we may attempt to manipulate the Holy Spirit for reputation (*see Acts 5:1-11).* Ananias and Sapphira participated in deliberate, deceitful, and demonic manipulation rooted in their motivation to be like Barnabas (*Acts 4:37*). They wanted a halo without holiness. As a result, they were both taken by God. Courting God and his Spirit for the benefit of one's reputation is dangerous and deadly business. You don't have to be eloquent, clever, sensational, or logical, but you must be real. If you are not real, you incalculably damage the cause that you represent.

Finally, we may attempt to manipulate the Holy Spirit through commercialization (*see Acts 8:9-24*). Here we find Simon the Sorcerer trying to buy the gifts of God. The gifts of God are not for sale for they are grace gifts. It would be a terrible miscalculation to believe that what we collect materially can take the place of the power of the Holy Spirit in our midst. Further, what a travesty to propose that we can buy or conjure up the gifts of the Holy Spirit. G. Campbell Morgan once said, "There is a lack in the church that can mean power, but there is a possession in the church that can mean paralysis."

An old preacher was asked by one of his church members to explain *John 3:8 ("The wind blows wherever it pleases....)*. "Tell me about the wind," the church member stated. The old preacher responded, "I don't know about the wind. All I know is that when the wind blows, we better hoist our sails and catch it." We cannot dictate the blow of the wind for this is a sovereign act. But, we can hoist our sails. The wind of God is a powerful symbol in scripture for his hidden depth and breadth of regenerating power. Did you know that both in Hebrew (Old Testament) and in Greek (New Testament) the terms for "spirit" and "wind" are the same? Consider the beauty of *Genesis 2:7* and *John 20:22: "The Lord God formed the man from the dust of the ground and breathed into his nostrils the breath of life, and the man became a living being...And Jesus breathed on them and said, 'Receive the Holy Spirit.' "*

Consider our chief example, Jesus (the head of the church). Jesus emptied himself and stepped out of heaven taking on the form of a man. *"And as he [Jesus] was praying, heaven was opened and the Holy Spirit descended on him in bodily form like a dove. And a voice came from heaven: 'You are my Son, whom I love; with you I am well pleased" (Luke 3:22)*. Notice *Luke 4:1* which reads, *"Jesus, full of the Holy Spirit..."* Contemplate his steady reliance upon the Spirit. *"Jesus returned to Galilee in the power of the Spirit..." (Luke 4:14)*. *John 3:34* captures our attention as John the Baptist characterizes Jesus. *"For the one whom God has sent speaks the words of God, for God gives the Spirit without limit [measure]."* Don't miss this principle which is intertwined through these scriptures. All that Jesus did, he did in the supernatural power of the Holy Spirit and this is the way that God desires for us to function.

Let me cut to the chase! The church is desperate for God's Spirit and his gifts to blow like a rushing wind and dancing fire. I believe he is ready! Is your church ready for such an experience? Disinterest, suspicion, and lack of knowledge concerning spiritual gifts fill most churches. Christian Schwarz's Natural Church Development Institute recently surveyed 1,200 Christians throughout the world. The results were shocking. Eighty percent of those surveyed had no idea what their spiritual gifts might be. Only twenty percent indicated that they knew what their spiritual gifts were and used them.[96] Take a moment to consider the implications of this survey's results. We are in the midst of a critical spiritual dilemma. The church can no longer treat the Spirit's presence and his gifts like power windows, antilock braking systems, or an airbag—merely options. A cafeteria style understanding of the Spirit of God and his gifts is rampant throughout the lands. Too many have bought into a form of church life today that suggests that the superstars do the work and the people pay and pray for the services.

Before we can progress, some scriptural reminders of God's gift(s) to us is at hand. The Bible does not lock us into tight restrictions as to the number of spiritual gifts or even their definitions. The four major lists of gifts are found in *Romans 12:3-8, I Corinthians 12:1-11,27-31,* and *Ephesians 4:11-12, I Peter 4:9-11,* but there are other passages that mention or illustrate gifts not included in these lists. God's grace (*charis*) undergirds all the gifts (*charismata*) of the Spirit (*Romans 12:6a, I Corinthians 12:4, I Peter 4:10*). The gifts, therefore, are rooted in God's grace (a free favor from God for the undeserving). Every believer has at least one gift (*I Corinthians 7:7*) and no one receives all the gifts (*I Corinthians 12:27-30*). If you had all the spiritual gifts, then you would have no need for anyone else in the body of Christ. And, no single gift is given to everyone (*I Corinthians 12:29-30*). Why? God is a God of variety. The Holy Spirit apportions the gifts to believers as he desires; you cannot earn a spiritual gift (*Ephesians 4:7*). If you could earn a gift, then what you earned wouldn't be a gift. As God graces you with a gift, the responsibility rests with you for the ensuing expression of the gift (*I Corinthians 12:11*).

God releases spiritual gifts to individuals in order to strengthen and edify the body of Christ. *"It was He who 'gave gifts to men'...to build up the Body of Christ so we shall all come together to that oneness in our faith...and become mature...Then we shall no longer be children, carried by the waves and blown about by every shifting wind..." (Ephesians 4:11, 13-14 GN).* The hoarding of one's spiritual gift(s) impairs the church from functioning as God has designed. The flaunting of spiritual gift(s) dishonors God, placing him a distant second to the members of the body. *"The Holy Spirit displays God's power through each of us as a means of helping the entire church" (I Corinthians 12:7 LB).* The appropriate and biblical usage of God's gift(s) to you and me provides power to the church.

With this scriptural backdrop, I would encourage you to consider God's designed connection between relationships and spiritual gifts. Let's consider one relationship in the scripture—Paul's relationship with his protege, Timothy. In his second letter to Timothy (who is now pastoring in Ephesus), Paul is reflecting upon this relationship. *"Night and day I constantly remember you in my prayers...I long to see you so that I might be filled with joy" (2 Timothy 1:3-4).* Paul blesses Timothy's mother and grandmother. He knows Timothy's family of origin. Because of Paul's relational connection with Timothy and his family, he pens some words of encouragement. Why was Timothy in need of encouragement? No one really knows. Maybe he was fearful, insecure, or experiencing relational conflict. Paul writes to Timothy, *"I remind you to fan into flame the gift of God, which is in you through the laying on of my hands" (2 Timothy 1:6).* This gift that Timothy is reminded of by Paul is rooted in God's grace. This special grace gift was received by Timothy to fully equip him for his pastoral responsibilities. Paul is saying to Timothy, "Stir up your gift! Remember your call, your vision to what God has commissioned you to accomplish through his grace." General Booth once stated, "The tendency of fire is to go out; watch the fire on the altar of your heart."

Paul continues: *"For God did not give us a spirit of timidity, but a spirit of power, of love and of elf-discipline" (2 Timothy 1:7).* In effect, Paul is reminding Timothy that God's power will enable him. He highlights in this word of encouragement God's love for Timothy. Further, Paul reminds Timothy that God provides his ultimate edification through self-discipline ("sound mind"). What are the results of this stirring of the gift? Timothy would be enabled by God's power, embraced by his love, and edified by his health and wholeness. My hunch is that Timothy received this gift of encouragement from Paul, his earthly mentor. Why? He knew Paul. He traveled with Paul. Paul laid his hands on him imparting "the gift of God." He had a vital, life giving relationship with Paul.

Spiritual gifts flow effectively through the conduit of relationships. Further, there is no greater place in the life of the church to experience God's release of the gifts than in a cell (remember the definition? "a set of relationships"). Paul Ford explains,

> Cell life is defined best as the place where God's grace in each member is revealed in their relationships. God has prepared things here as well! He has given each of us an 'oikos,' a network of relationships including extended family, friends and associates just as he planned. As the New Testament Christian lived out his faith in his oikos, or network of relationships, so are each of us called to be faithful stewards of our relationships. In fact, Peter actually uses the word 'oikonomos,' which literally means "relationship manager" in the Greek. We are called to be faithful stewards of those whom God gives us.
>
> Here is God's remarkable plan for humankind, simplified into your cell group setting: He pours out His grace on our lives unto salvation. Then He gives each of us a portion of His grace so that together we can build up one another and reveal that grace to a world of lost souls. Finally, He gives each of us relationships with non-Christians and fallen away Christians, challenging us to be good stewards of those strategic relationships by investing our grace gifts.[97]

A few examples will allow one to "feel" this connection between ministering in one's giftedness via relationships. Mike and Laurie were struggling in their marriage. They opened up their marital challenges and conflicts with their cell members during their weekly gathering. The cell members allowed God's grace to flow through them, listened intently, shed some tears, and placed Mike and Laurie in the middle of their circle laying hands on them as they covered this struggling couple with prayer. Immediately, two ladies in this cell began to meet with Laurie providing ministry, encouragement, and support. The grace gifts of God were being poured out on Laurie. She knew that she was not alone and received the support with an open heart and mind. Concurrently, a few men in this cell began to meet frequently with Mike. The men were able to discern Mike's anger rooted in past hurts. Mike confessed his sin of raging against his wife and children. He desperately wanted to change but admittedly needed accountability and continual counsel. The men supported Mike and his desire to be free from rage. Weekly, Mike and these men would meet for prayer and intercession.

Despite the gifts that God poured out through these cell members to Mike and Laurie, the marital conflict increased. Yet, the cell members did not give up! They prayed, babysat their children, provided money for overdue bills, and a car was given so that Mike might have a vehicle for work. Mike and Laurie were completely surrounded by cell members who were lavishing God's grace gifts upon them. As time progressed, Mike confessed his independent spirit. He repeatedly would receive counsel from the men in his cell and then respond in a destructive manner. Laurie determined in her heart that she no longer loved Mike and wanted out of the marriage. The cell members did not give up! Regular intercession gatherings were planned and the cell members collected money to pay for extensive marriage counseling. Mike and Laurie received marriage counseling, and their marriage looked like it would prevail.

As the weeks progressed, however, Mike and Laurie allowed the enemy to destroy their relationship. They both agreed to divorce. My guess is that you were anticipating a different outcome. You are not alone. The deterioration of Mike and Laurie's marriage broke the hearts of the cell members. At one cell gathering, the room was filled with a strong presence of grief, despair, and hopelessness. The hearts were heavy...and then God showed up. During a time of prayer, God's gift of encouragement filled one cell member, and he spoke about God's heart for Mike and Laurie. Once again, the cell members did not give up! It would have been easy to cast blame and judgment upon Mike and Laurie. It would have been convenient to recall all the time, effort, energy and money that the cell members provided to this young couple. It would have been easy to wallow in their disappointment, anger, and hurt. But, God's gift of encouragement lifted this group to continue to express God's grace and love to Mike and Laurie. This is precisely what has taken place.

Although Mike and Laurie are no longer married, they both have experienced extreme brokenness and godly sorrow for their failed marriage. Specifically, the men of the cell who ministered to Mike were recently reminded that the "Word of the Lord never returns empty or void." Mike asked for a meeting with the two gentlemen who supported him and confessed his independence, deceit, pride, and refusal to receive God's gifts of love and counsel. God got a hold of Mike's heart of stone and made it into a heart of flesh. Today, Mike is changed, different and filled with the Holy Spirit. Bondages and root spirits have been broken in his life. Certainly, the consequences for Mike's divorce cannot be eradicated, but God and his people did not give up on Mike. Today, Mike leads a cell at CCC. Why? Because God broke his heart and he accepted God's forgiveness, and resolved to be a disciple of Christ. Further, God used ordinary men to come alongside Mike and be conduits of God's grace gifts.

I want you to notice a few things about this scenario in Mike and Laurie's life. Notice who they turned to in the midst of a crisis. Yes, that's right. They turned to a safe set of relationships—the men and women in their cell. Further, notice who God used to minister to this couple. Ordinary people—housewives and businessmen. Did you notice that Mike and Laurie didn't immediately run to their pastor? No, God ministered his grace gifts through an established set of relationships.

My friends, Todd and Abby, are tremendously talented and gifted shepherds of a cell at CCC. A few days ago, I received an email from Todd in which the subject line was entitled, "God at Work!" Needless to say, this caught my attention and I opened the email and read it with great joy. At a cell gathering, Abby shared her concern and compassion with the cell about a couple that was struggling in a very severe way. The young man was literally dying due to a self imposed intake of pills and alcohol. In his drunken stupor, he began to call a few of his cell members for help. He knew who to turn to! He knew who really loved him. As his last minutes were fleeing, a friend found him and was able to contact the authorities and medical personnel. He was immediately admitted to the hospital for substance abuse, depression, and attempted suicide. Concurrently, his wife was without food for the children and life seemed unmanageable.

Abby asked for the cell members to come alongside this young couple so that they might "get back on their feet." As Abby was talking and explaining that the cell needed to try and find a way to come up with about $1000.00 to help pay their bills and buy some groceries, someone just started passing a hat around the circle. When the monies in the hat were totaled, $1431.00 had been collected to help this hurting couple. The next day, Todd called the young man who had just been released from the hospital and shared the cell's intent to be used by God to help and restore. The young man was filled with such gratitude that Todd described him as "one who was both in shock and choking back tears." In his email to me, Todd writes, "Rob, in all my years as a Christian, NEVER have I seen God at work like I have the last several years. What an experience! What an awesome ride!" Indeed, Todd and Abby are enjoying ministry because God is releasing his gifts through them and their fellow cell members.

Scott was also a part of this cell gathering. Ponder these words that he expressed to Todd via email the very next day.

> Last night's cell gathering was awesome. God is doing something big every week. I just wanted to let you know what I saw last night as an interested observer. First, you should know that your wife is a very special person. She was telling us about the young couple's situation with a sound of desperation in her voice. Indeed, it sounds like a truly desperate situation. While she was

talking, I was seeing in my mind the church in the book of Acts. There was one church in the city for Celebration and the people met regularly in small groups in people's homes meeting one another's needs. Abby said that she didn't want to take this to the pastors, but the cell should deal with it.

About the third time she said, "I don't know what to do..." Chuck took some cash out of his pocket and handed it to Trevor. Trevor added something to it and handed the wad of cash to Mike. Mike looked confused. Trevor took off his hat, put the wad of cash in the hat and handed it to Mike. Mike added something and passed it on. The hat was half way around the room before Abby even knew what was happening. She was still looking for suggestions.

The bottom line here is that it's not us, but it's not just the Holy Spirit either. He is working in our lives and we respond. In this case, Chuck took the first step. Nobody stood up and said, "Listen to Abby, we should pass a hat and see what we can do." Chuck responded to God as it says in James—with faith-based action. I am so humbled to be in this group. And so excited at the same time.

My friends, let me confess that I had nothing to do with either of these powerful stories. The ministry to these two couples was accomplished through ordinary individuals who responded to God's call and faithfully utilized their gifts from God and allowed God's gifts to flow. Although I was not an eyewitness to these ministry encounters, I can compile a list of gifts that were released by God in these situations. This list would include (but not be limited to) mercy, exhortation, discernment, giving, intercession, administration, counseling, faith, teaching, helps, hospitality, and shepherding. This team approach of gift-oriented ministry leaves no one individual carrying the full weight of ministering into the lives of others. On the contrary, when an individual is ministering in his giftedness, he experiences fruitfulness and fulfillment.

Now, multiply these gift-oriented ministry scenarios by one hundred....two hundred....one thousand. Think of how ordinary individuals who are filled with God's Spirit and ministering in their giftedness can affect your church, city, country and world. Think of the dancing fire of God's Spirit that is available and ready to be released. Think of how these Spirit-filled cells are experiencing *Ephesians 2:22: "And in Him you too are being built together to become a dwelling in which God lives by His Spirit."*

Let me take you back to that youth retreat where I received an unsolicited life lesson on fire and ashes. Sit down here next to me. As you glance toward the horizon, you see hundreds of young people leaving an incredible weekend filled with God's fire. You're not on the bus. You want to be on the bus. Your mind wanders as you contemplate, "What are they doing on the bus?" You are sitting next to my buddy Mark and me—watching smoldering ashes. I can tell you just like it was yesterday—that job is no fun! It is boring. You desire to get on with life; to return to your home. No, you must watch what was once a dancing fire transform into a pile of burnt up ashes. My friend, I implore you—Don't settle for smoldering ashes! Go to God and ask him to *"fan into flame the gift of God."*

Chapter Twelve

"Let's Roll"

*I*t was Monday and my week began at a rapid pace. I lifted my body out of bed, showered and headed for an early morning gathering. The gathering drew to a close and I darted to CCC's "Living Room" (Worship Center) to lead a few equipping sessions for fifty Korean pastors who were in Wimberley investigating the church. As early afternoon approached, I excused myself, turned these wonderful Korean friends over to the CCC pastoral team, and headed for my daughter's volleyball game in Ingram, Texas. I don't miss her games. I love the drive time with my wife and youngest daughter. Further, I enjoy watching Taylor pursue and develop as an athlete. After a quick bite to eat, we returned to our home and began the nightly preparations of getting the kids to bed.

The next morning, I was in my home office, preparing to meet again with the Korean pastors and then catch an early afternoon flight to Baton Rouge. It was early, and my preparation was momentarily interrupted when the phone rang. My friend, Jim, was on the phone and abruptly asked me a question (with a sense of urgency). "Rob, are you watching T.V.?" "No," I responded. "Jim, how are you? What's going on?" "Never mind me," he stated, "Turn on the T.V. now!" "What channel?" I asked and the phone went dead. Now I have received some strange phone calls in my life, but what was up with Jim? Jim is a former policeman and I heeded his command by casually retrieving the remote control and turning on the T.V.

It was Tuesday, September 11, 2001. There I stood frozen before the nine inch television screen in my office. I need not divulge the tragic events that were unfolding. Ninety-nine percent of the world's population understand the events surrounding "9-11." Racing through my home, I turned another T.V. on so that my wife could watch the horrific pictures at the World Trade Center.

The minutes quickly passed, and I left for the gathering with Paul Jeong and my other Korean friends. As small groups of our Korean guests began to arrive at the church building, my heart was heavy watching these dear friends weep for America. A sweet time of prayer, worship and repentance ensued. The Koreans were now leading the gathering and that was good. Certainly, their gift to the world wide body of Christ has been and remains heartfelt intercession and prayer. Anything that was to be presented by the pastors of CCC paled in comparison to this time of prayer and the events of the day. As the time of prayer ended, I noticed our local newspaper editor was in our midst. Paul and I answered a few questions for "Mac" and then I paused. What a difference one day makes! Black Tuesday changed me, my fellow Americans, and millions throughout the world. America was in a state of shock, stunned by the devastating loss of life at the Twin Towers and Pentagon.

Americans were encouraged by President Bush to pray as he pledged to rid the world of evil. On Friday, September 15, 2001, millions throughout America gathered in churches for a time of prayer, repentance, and remembrance. I will not soon forget the hundreds of people from the community that came to CCC on that somber day to seek God's peace, to pray for friends who were missing in the rubble, and to ask God for protection and direction for America and in their own personal lives. For the very first time, many Americans realized their own nation's vulnerability. America had been attacked, and a war to eradicate terrorism around the world was soon to ensue.

The continual footage and videotape feed from the media enabled every American to experience the collapse of the Twin Towers and the incredible damage levied against the Pentagon. One network anchor stated, "Think of it, our two symbols of power and prosperity have been smitten in one hour." The hearts of the American people were broken, and the immediate return to God's heart was encouraging. Indeed, the time was ripe for God's dancing hand to move across the country as people flocked to churches. Yes, God is the only one who could turn such heartache, brokenness, and unbelief into something good. God was providing every church a possibility to extend care and comfort to the trouble-hearted. With no doubt, many lives were touched by the grace and mercy of God. Many churches were ready, sleek, and responsive. Specifically, many pastors in this region reported an immediate thirty percent increase in worship attendance. Overall, however, "churches succeeded at putting on a friendly face but failed at motivating the vast majority of spiritual explorers to connect with Christ in a more intimate or intense manner."[98]

Using twenty-one indicators of the nation's spiritual climate, the Barna Research Group revealed a comprehensive report at how America's faith changed in the aftermath of 9-11. This report states,

Church volunteerism, after an initial outpouring of involvement, is back at pre-attack levels (23% invest some time in church-related service during a typical week). It adds that, despite assumptions to the contrary, prayer is 'currently at its normal level, with 85% praying to God in a given week.' Fewer people believe in an all-knowing God and fewer believe in Satan as a real person, rather they see him now as a symbol of evil.

After the attack, millions of nominally churched or generally irreligious Americans were desperately seeking something that would restore stability and a sense of meaning to life. Fortunately, many of them turned to the church. Unfortunately, few of them experienced anything that was sufficiently life-changing to capture their attention and their allegiance. They tended to appreciate the moments of comfort they received, but were unaware of anything sufficiently unique or beneficial as to redesign their lifestyle to integrate a deeper level of spiritual involvement.

The September 11 tragedy was another amazing

opportunity for churches to be the healing and transforming presence of God in people's lives, but that, too, has
now come and gone, with little to show for it. After the 9-
11 attacks, religious activity surged, but within two
months, virtually every spiritual indicator available
suggested that things were back to pre-attack levels.[99]

Most assuredly, it would be unfair to proscribe complete fault
upon the various churches throughout the country, for there are
many factors that lead to a changed life—mainly, the pliability of
one's heart coupled with a desire to receive the hope and love of
God. While this is true, I do believe that the majority of folks who
returned to the church were highly "under-whelmed." For the most
part, life transformation was not experienced, and the general heart
of America's spirituality remained unchanged.

In reality, these post "9-11" results are indicative of a tremendous slump that has been apparent over the last decade. As an
example, the American Religious Identification Survey offers a
statistical snapshot of believers and seekers in order to predict what
the future may hold. Egon Mayer and Barry Kosmin were the lead
investigators for the study funded by the Graduate Center of the
City University of New York. This 2001 survey of more than
50,000 adults weaves a "mesmerizing tapestry of faith groups" and
a growing number who reject the religion label.[100] The following
data reveals the growth rates for the largest denominations in
America, and those who say they do not align with any denomina-
tion or religion, from 1990 to 2001.

Christian Religions	2001	Percent Change
Catholic	50,873,000	10.6%
Baptist	33,830,000	-0.4%
Christian (no denomination supplied)	14,190,000	75.8%
Methodist/Wesleyan	14,140,000	-0.2%
Lutheran	9,580,000	5.2%
Presbyterian	5,596,000	12.3%
Pentecostal/Charismatic	4,407,000	38.1%

Assemblies of God	1,106,000	67.6%

Non-Christian Religions	2001	Percent Change
Muslim/Islamic	1,104,000	109.5%
Buddhist	1,082,000	169.8%
Hindu	766,000	237.4%
Unitarian/Universalist	629,000	25.3%
Wiccan	134,000	1,575%
No Religion	29,481,000	105.7%

(includes atheist, agnostic, humanist, secular)

The American church has been losing ground for years as more and more individuals are migrating to non-Christian religions or are proclaiming themselves to have no religion persuasion or affiliation.

Meshing the events surrounding "9-11" with the message and principles revealed in this book is a daunting task for any writer. I would, however, like to ponder the implications of this event through the lenses of the Bible, history, and the specific principles of church health that have formed the backdrop for this book. I will pluck principles from these three lenses that should grant to every reader caution, hope, anticipation, and a deep desire for God to work in an unprecedented way in the American church.

Let's begin by discovering some principles from God's Word. Without a doubt, a key question that was asked around cafes, living rooms, conference centers, institutes of higher learning, and more was "Where is God in all this?" This is an understandable question and should be pondered. Chances are strong that no single human being who strives to bring understanding to the presented question can adequately appease everyone who asked this question. I do believe, however, that God was not taken by surprise by "9-11." He is not wringing his hands in heaven wondering how such evil could be present in the world. He is sovereign, knowing the hearts of all men and women. We also know that never in history has God left his people clueless in a time of calamity. *"He will never leave or forsake you."* In other words, he is not leaving us alone in our sorrow and anguish forcing us to figure out things on our own. He is willing, able and ready to dispense his wisdom to all who may ask.

Further, he is a God who draws near to the broken-hearted. He is a God who "does" sorrow.

An example from the people of God, the Israelites, will help. During Isaiah's ministry, God had been dealing patiently with Israel for approximately 250 years. Despite this prophet's continual warnings and encouragement for Israel to return to God, inevitably "God's people" rejected God, continually thumbing their noses at him. *"The Israelites secretly did things against the Lord their God that were not right" (2 Kings 17:9).* The Bible records numerous prophets over the ages encouraging Israel to "humble themselves" and return to their Maker and Creator. *"...They did wicked things that provoked the Lord to anger. They worshiped idols, though the Lord had said, 'You shall not do this.' The Lord warned Israel and Judah through all his prophets and seers: 'Turn from your evil ways. Observe my commands and decrees, in accordance with the entire Law that I commanded you fathers to obey and that I delivered to you through my servants the prophets' " (2 Kings 17:11b-13).* The people of Israel *"would not listen and were as stiff necked as their fathers, who did not trust in the Lord their God" (2 Kings 17:14).*

Because of these actions, the Lord sent two wake up calls to the Israelites. The first wake up call came through an Assyrian invasion upon the provinces of Zebulun and Naphtali. These attacks rattled the heart of God's people, but it ultimately did not change their hearts. The second wake up call came through Israel's two chief enemies, the Syrians and the Philistines. Combining forces, these nations came from the east and west and completely surrounded Israel inflicting immense devastation. This coalition of enemy nations wreaked havoc upon Israel as their buildings collapsed and fires raged. *"The Lord has sent a message against Jacob; it will fall on Israel. All the people will know it—Ephraim and the inhabitants of Samaria—who say with pride and arrogance of heart, 'The bricks have fallen down, but we will rebuild with dressed stone; the fig trees have been felled, but we will replace them with cedars' " (Isaiah 9:8-10).* One must understand that God will use enemy nations to chasten his people.

In the midst of this calamity, Israel had one of two choices to make. First, they could choose to repent and humble themselves before God. They could return to God and live in his provision and blessing. However, this was not their choice! Instead, they turned to their own strength and ingenuity decisively taking matters into their own hands. This choice resulted in deeper desolation, destruction, and separation from God. Ultimately, Israel was disciplined by God.

With great certainty, America received an incredible wake up call in the context of national security. The heart of our nation has been crushed, but not broken. Examining the parallel principles to the scenarios faced by the Israelites in the past is warranted. Yet, I stop short in suggesting that God is doing the same thing with this nation as he did with the nation of Israel. God allowed this calamity to strike, but for what reason? I will allow another, more prolific writer and pastor to postulate on this matter. I do know that any objective observer would be quick to embrace repentance and wholeheartedly cry out, "God, we need you. Cleanse our hearts, purify us. We will return to you. We cannot make it without you." As Americans have gathered in a myriad of ceremonies post "9-11," more questions need to be presented. Do we really trust God to deliver us from the hands of evil? Or, can we as a nation carry on relying solely on our own strength, patriotism, ingenuity, wealth, and dominance? We would be wise to heed the prophets of the ages counsel to Israel: "Humble yourselves and return to God."

The churches of this nation had an incredible opportunity to extend the kingdom of God in this land. Without any doubt, the church was not ready, nor prepared, for such a time as this!

Because judgment begins with the house of God, let's put on the second set of lenses and take an abbreviated historical look at the church over the ages. Specifically, let's compare the first three-hundred years of the church with today's church. To accomplish this task, let's turn to Jon Zens and his excellent writing, *The Four Tragic Shifts in the Visible Church*, which will certainly aid us in this journey. Zens writes,

> While there are a legion of disagreements among serious students of church history concerning various issues and details during the period of 50 A.D. to 325 A.D., they all speak as one voice in affirming four undeniable shifts.

Church historians of all theological and ecclesiastical backgrounds observe in their writings the following four shifts:

1. The church portrayed in the New Testament was a dynamic organism, a living body with many parts. The church from around 180 A.D. onwards became an increasingly hardened institution with a fixed and complex hierarchy.

2. The early church was marked by the manifestation of a polyform ministry by which edification and the meeting of needs were accomplished through the gifts of all the brethren. The post-apostolic church moved more and more toward a uniform conception of church offices which separated ministry from the 'laity' and limited significant ministry to the 'clergy'.

3. The church of the first and most of the second centuries was characterized by cycles of intense difficulty and persecution—it was a suffering body. With the advent of Constantine the church became protected, favored and ultimately sanctioned as the state religion by the Romans state, and thus became an institution at ease.

4. The New Testament church, with no small measure of vulnerability, depended on the Holy Spirit to hold the brethren together and to lead them in ministry. Later, the church trusted in itself as a very powerful institution, along with its many rules, rites and offices to secure visible unity among its adherents.[101]

With these four tragic shifts in the life of the church as a backdrop, one should not be surprised at the post "9-11" report cited previously by the Barna Research Group. The American church is but a microcosm of these shifts that have influenced the world wide church. Specifically, we have preempted a living, multi-bodied

organism with rigid structure and hierarchy. We have institutional-
ized the church fitting her with "offices," all the while, supplanting
and suppressing the gifts of the body. Further, embracing the persecution suffered by the early church is a distant thought to us today
despite the many men and women who gave their lives for the cause
of Christ throughout the centuries. Finally, the flow of God's Spirit
has been repressed in favor of a cosmetic, surface appearance of
unity through religion, rules, and regulations.

The post "9-11" results could and should have been different.
The significance of Black Tuesday must be understood through the
first two lenses (Biblical and historical perspective) I have just
discussed. The tragic devastation, the heart breaking loss of thousands of lives, and the very present danger of soldiers and fellow
countrymen is undeniably difficult, if not impossible, to absorb. In
no way should one minimize this tragic day. I certainly am not and
will not. However, let me cut to the chase. How will we (the
American church) respond to such an occurrence? Will we carry on
being who we have been in the past? Will we utilize the same
methodology of "building the church?" Can we be used of God to
bridge the gap between hopelessness, fear, despair and a loving
God filled with hope and life?

Let's imagine a different scenario in the crucial days and weeks
that followed "9-11." Imagine the millions who flocked to churches
throughout the land and discovered a multi-faceted, well connected
body of Christ teeming with life and love. Imagine millions finding
hope in Jesus Christ through the thousands of lighthouses dotting the
landscape. Imagine the tears of repentance that would flow, the
joyous laughter as people discovered they really were loved by God,
and the permeating hope that would capture the entire nation. The
collective consciousness of one nation truly under God would have
revolutionized our country and world. But, this did not occur. Why?
This question leads to the third and final lens; specifically, the principles of church health that have been highlighted in this book.

The current disenchantment with the church growth movement
present in the last two decades is blatantly evident among American
pastors. Taking time to recount the numerous lessons learned during
the church growth movement would be laborious, and ultimately,

unprofitable. Let me cite, however, three simple lessons that we have learned. First, we have learned that church growth does not necessarily mean that a church is healthy. Next, the majority of church growth techniques seem to have tarnished, rather than enhanced, the bride of Christ. Finally, we learned afresh and anew that Jesus builds his church. When Jesus builds, the fruit remains. When Jesus builds, health permeates the members. When Jesus builds, contentment resides and abides. When Jesus builds, all men, women, young people, and children are drawn to him.

My desire is not to begrudge the past or curse where we have come from. No, not at all! Rather, let's move forward to a refreshing and freeing philosophical outlook that brings forth HEALTHY New Testament churches. Let's embrace the reality that health precedes growth. Let's move and flow in the essential characteristics of a healthy church that I have adopted from Christian Schwarz as a general backdrop for this book (Passionate Spirituality, Loving Relationships, Need-Oriented Evangelism, Holistic Small Groups/Cells, Inspiring Worship, Empowering Leadership, Gift-Oriented Ministry, and Functional Structures).

I admitted in the Preface of this book that these eight essential characteristics of a healthy church would be transmitted to you via the power of stories. I trust that through these stories, the Holy Spirit has birthed in you an appetite to pursue health, individually and corporately, as we collectively seek to become a church that is ready, full of life, actively pursuing the Great Commandment and Great Commission.

This pursuit requires two things. First, we must choose to abandon our comfort in "how <u>WE</u> do church." Today's church is decades behind the ever evolving and fascinating shifts in the culture. Spiritually, we are empty. Corporately, we are divided. We are in deep need of God's dancing hand in our midst. Second, we must choose to RISK and embrace change in order to extend the kingdom of God!

God gave to us through "9-11" thousands of stories of individuals who abandoned their own personal comfort and risked their very lives. My assumption is that volumes could be filled with such stories. One would be hard pressed to find a more moving illustration of the virtues of abandoning comfort and choosing to risk than a man named Todd Beamer.

Todd was a passenger on United Airlines Flight 93 that departed from Newark, New Jersey at 8:42 AM on Tuesday, September 11, 2001. Unbeknown to Todd upon his departure from Newark, he was going to be used by God to make an indelible mark upon a country and world. Accompanying Todd and the other passengers and crew members, were three or four terrorists led by Ziad Samir Jarrah, who desired to wreak havoc and destruction upon an American landmark by hijacking this commercial airliner. However, these "hijackers of United Airlines 93 didn't bank on the plane's passengers banding together to take them on. By charging the cockpit, these heroes prevented the plane from crashing into the nation's capital—where it seemed to be headed."[102]

Eighteen minutes following the flight's departure from Newark, the plane reached cruising altitude. At this time, the pilots were warned by United Airlines of possible cockpit intrusion. This information was given to the pilots based on the circumstances surrounding American Airlines Flight 11 and United Airlines Flight 175 which crashed into the North and South Towers of the World Trade Center. Approximately thirty minutes later, the cockpit of Flight 93 was charged by Jarrah and his evil comrades. A controller at the Cleveland Ohio airport terminal heard one of the pilots yelling, "Get out of here, get out of here."[103] Within minutes, the passengers and flight attendants were forced to move to the back of the plane.

At 9:36 AM, the plane made an abrupt, hairpin turn west of Cleveland and began to head in a southeast direction for the nation's capital. At this point, the flight attendants and passengers began to plot a plan to preserve their lives. Numerous passengers used their cell phones to call loved ones and seek out help. Through a bizarre circumstance, Todd utilized his cell phone and was connected to Lisa Jefferson, a supervisor for the GTE Customer Center in Oakbrook, Illinois. "In a calm and businesslike way, Todd rattled off the details (3 hijackers, 2 with knives; 10 passengers in first class, 27 in coach, 5 flight attendants; no children that he could see)."[104]

At approximately 9:58 AM, the crew members and flight

attendants decided to charge the cockpit in an effort to overtake the hijackers. "Oh, my God," said Todd [to Jefferson], "I don't think we're going to get out of this thing. I'm going to have to go out on faith."[105] Todd received Jefferson's assurance that she would contact Todd's wife, Lisa. He informed her of his two boys and the new baby yet to be born. Before disconnecting with Jefferson, Todd asked her to pray with him as he recited the Lord's Prayer. "Jesus help me," he said. He recited the 23rd Psalm. Then Jefferson heard him say: "Are you guys ready? Let's ROLL."[106] Todd and his fellow passengers raced 110 feet from the rear of the plane to the cockpit. Six to eight minutes later, United Airlines Flight 93 crashed into a Somerset County, Pennsylvania field. The crater in the field was fifty feet deep after it hit. Todd, his fellow passengers, the flight crew, and the hijackers were killed instantly upon impact.

As the weeks unfolded following Todd's heroic death, Lisa (his wife) journeyed into the den of the Beamer home. It was on Todd's desk that she found, on a folded piece of paper, a passage quoting Teddy Roosevelt:

> The credit belongs to the man who is actually in the arena...who strives valiantly, who knows the great enthusiasms, the great devotions, and spends himself in worthy causes. Who, at best, knows the triumph of high achievement and who, at worst, if he fails, fails while daring greatly so that his place shall never be with those cold and timid souls who know neither victory nor defeat.[107]

Is there any greater model than Todd Beamer who chose to abandon his own comfort and risk his life? Actually, yes. Many have done so over the course of history. Yet, the greatest model of abandonment and risk remains to this day—Jesus Christ. He stepped out of the comfort of heaven to show us the love of God. He risked being God with skin on in the midst of religious persecution and tyrannical rule. He risked being a fulfillment to the Law. He risked by loving the unlovely. He risked by charging his disciples to receive the power of the Holy Spirit and spread the gospel to all nations. Jesus knows about leaving comfortable settings and risk.

This abandonment of comfort and risk led him to a cross where he gave his life for all the world. He gave his life so that the church might be filled with life. Most assuredly, we can receive inspiration and hope as we choose to be captivated by this model of abandonment and risk. This was true of Todd Beamer who knew Jesus Christ as friend, Lord and Savior. He was emulating the greatest hero of all time—Jesus Christ.

Will you "spend yourself in a worthy cause?" Will you know the "triumph of high achievement?" Will you "dare greatly" so that the church of Jesus Christ will be changed?

Will you *dance with Daddy* [our great, Abba Father]? Will you be a part of his great dance throughout the world? My friends, let's take off the shackles and dance! My friends, let's abandon our comfort and risk our lives for the cause of Christ. My friends, "Let's ROLL!"

Endnotes

1 Institute for Natural Church Development.

2 *Christianity Today*, April 3, 2000

3 Church Resource Ministry, Inc., Sam Metcalf

4 Church Planting Ministries, Jim Allen

5 "Church Membership" *San Antonio Express News* (17 February 2001): 9b.

6 Institute for Natural Church Development

7 US Center for World Mission, Patrick Johnstone & David Barrett

8 Sweet, Leonard. *Soul Tsunami* (Grand Rapids, MI: Zondervan Publishing House, 1999), 254.

9 Luther, Martin, *Table Talk*, no. 5047, in *Luther's Works*, ed. And trans. Theodore G. Tappert (Philadelphia: Fortress Press, 1967), 54:383-4.

10 Crabb, Larry. *The Silence of Adam: Becoming Men of Courage in a World of Chaos* (Grand Rapids, MI: Zondervan Publishing House, 1995), 75.

11 Ibid, 101.

12 Sweet, Leonard. *Soul Tsuanami: Sink or Swim in New Millennium Culture* (Grand Rapids, MI: Zondervan Publishing House, 1999), 424.

13 Hunter, George C. *The Celtic Way of Evangelism* (Nashville, TN: Abingdon Press, 2000), 64.

14 Allen, Kathi, *The Art of Telling—and Listening to—Stories that Matter: An Interview with Dr. Daniel Taylor,* www.theooze.com, 7 Jan 2002.

15 As reported in *Sunday Mercury, Birmingham, UK* (17 December 2000).

16 Nash Jr., Robert. *An 8-Track Church in a CD World* (Macon, GA: Smyth & Helwys Publishing, Inc., 1997), 55.

17 Regele, Mike. *The Death of the Church* (Grand Rapids, MI: Zondervan), 20.

18 Woodward, Kenneth L., *"Dead End for the Mainline?" Newsweek* (9

August 1993): 46.

[19] Boomershine, Thomas E., *"The Polish Cavalry and Christianity in Electronic Culture," Journal of Theology* 95 (1995): 97-98.

[20] Tenney, Tommy. *The God Chasers* (Shippensburg, PA: Destiny Image Publishers, Inc., 1998), 2.

[21] Neighbour, Ralph W., *Introductory Cell Church Seminar* presented in Miami, FL, 1996 (Touch Outreach Ministries, Houston, TX), "Why the Holy Spirit Has Launched the Cell Church Movement," 2-3.

[22] Phillips, Donald T. *Lincoln on Leadership: Executive Strategies for Tough Times* (New York: Warner Books, 1992), 55-56.

[23] Sweet, Leonard. *Soul Tsunami* (Grand Rapids, MI: Zondervan Publishing House, 1999), 32.

[24] bid, 339.

[25] Cunningham, Lawrence. *Imaging Christ: Politics, Art, Spirituality* (Villanova, PA: Villanova University Press, 1991), 60.

[26] Sweet, 206.

[27] Hunter, George C. *The Celtic Way of Evangelism* (Nashville, TN: Abingdon Press, 2000), 97.

[28] bid., 97.

[29] Nash Jr., Robert. *8-Track Church in a CD World* (Macon, GA: Smith and Helwys Publishing, Inc., 1997), 131-132.

[30] When I use this word "culture," I prefer George C. Hunter's definition of culture *(The Celtic Way of Evangelism, p. 100)* which states: A culture is defined as the learned pattern of beliefs, attitudes, values, customs, and products shared by a people. A culture is sometimes explained, metaphorically, as "the software of the mind" that has been "programmed" into a given people's shared consciousness through their enculturation.

[31] Sweet, Leonard. *The Postmodern Pilgrims* (Nashville, TN: Broadman and Holman Publishers, 2000), 7.

[32] Frank E. Gaebelein, ed., *The Expositor's Bible Commentary* (Grand Rapids, MI: Zondervan Publishing House, 1985), Volume 7, 34-35.

[33] Schwarz, Christian. *Natural Church Development: A Guide to Eight Essential Qualities of Healthy Churches* (Carol Stream, IL: ChurchSmart Resources, 1998), 22.

[34] Peck, M. Scott. *A World Waiting to Be Born: Civility Rediscovered* (New York: Bantam Books, 1993), 268.

35 Maxwell, John, *Flying Geese of Florida,* "Leadership at Large," Vol. 4, Issue 24, p. 2.

36 Ibid, 4.

37 Brown, William, "Growing the Church Through Small Groups in the Australian Context," (D. Min. dissertation, Fuller Theological Seminary, 1992), 37.

38 Sweet, Leonard. *Soul Tsunami: Sink or Swim in New Millennium Culture* (Grand Rapids, MI: Zondervan Publishing House, 1999), 216.

39 Barna, George. *The Habits of Highly Effective Churches* (Ventura, CA: Regal Books, 1999), 46.

40 Sweet, 313.

41 Barna, 46.

42 Neal, Gail, "Faithfulness in the Heartland," accessed through www.gocn.org, June 1998, Vol. 10, No. 2 .

43 bid,

44 Clinton, J. Robert. *The Making of a Leader* (Colorado Springs, CO: Navpress, 1988), 14.

45 Blanchard, K.H. and Hersey, P. *Management of Organizational Behavior: Utilizing Human Resources* (Upper Saddle River, NJ: Prentice Hall, 1992), 5.

46 Depree, Max. *Leadership Is an Art* (New York: Doubleday, 1989), 10.

47 Barna, George. *The Second Coming of the Church* (Nashville, TN: Word Books, 1998), 106.

48 Barna, George. *The Index of Leading Spiritual Indicators* (Dallas: Word, 1996), 118.

49 Thrall, Bill. *The Ascent of a Leader* (San Francisco, CA: Jossey-Bass Publishers, 1999), 154.

50 Buford, Bob. *Half Time: Changing Your Game Plan from Success to Significance* (Grand Rapids, MI: Zondervan, 1994), 167.

51 Ibid, *The Habits of Highly Effective Churches* , 37.

52 Ibid, 32.

53 Sweet, Leonard. *Soul Tsunami: Sink or Swim in New Millennium Culture* (Grand Rapids, MI: Zondervan Publishing House, 1999), 306.

54 Finney, John. *Recovering the Past: Celtic and Roman Mission* (London: Darton, Longman and Todd Ltd., 1996).

55 Hunter, George C. *The Celtic Way of Evangelism* (Nashville, TN: Abingdon Press, 2000), 47.

[56] Ibid, 53.

[57] Finney, 67.

[58] Spader, Dann. *Growing a Healthy Church Manual* (Elburn, ILL: SonLife Publications, 1996), 28.

[59] Spader, Dann. *Growing a Healthy Church* (Chicago, ILL: Moody Press, 1991), 32.

[60] Ibid, 21.

[61] Bibby, Reginald, "Beyond Circulating the Saints," *Faith Today,* March-April 1990, 23.

[62] Finnell, David. *Life in His Body* (Houston, TX: Touch Publications, 1995), 75.

[63] Ibid, 76.

[64] Ibid, 79.

[65] Silvoso, Ed. *That None Should Perish* (Ventura, CA: Regal Books, 1994), 57.

[66] Spader, 47.

[67] Wilson, Carl. *With Christ in the School of Disciple Building* (Grand Rapids, MI: Zondervan, 1976), 223.

[68] Celek, Tim and Zander, Dieter. *Inside the Soul of a New Generation* (Grand Rapids, MI: Zondervan, 1996), 88.

[69] Ibid, 89.

[70] Allen, Kathy, *The Art of Telling—and Listening to—Stories that Matter: An Interview with Dr. Daniel Taylor,* www.theooze.com (7 January 2002).

[71] Ibid.

[72] Ibid, 76-77.

[73] Finney, John. *Finding Faith Today: How Does it Happen?* (British and Foreign Bible Society, 1992), 46.

[74] Phillips, Donald T. *Lincoln Stories for Leaders* (Arlington, TX: Summit Publishing Group, 1997), 16-17.

[75] Vega, Mario, "Cell Leadership in the Face of Tragedy," *Cell Group Journal*, Volume 10, Number 3 Summer 2001, 20.

[76] Ibid., 23.

[77] Collins, James C. and Porras, Jerry I. *Built to Last: Successful Habits of Visionary Companies* (New York, NY: Harper Business, 1997), 73.

[78] Piper, John, "When the Bridegroom is Taken Away," January 8, 1995, audiocassette.

79 Schwarz, Christian. *Implementation Guide to Natural Church Development* (Carol Stream, IL: Church Smart Resources, 1998), 176.

80 Reagan, David. *Living for Christ in the End Times* (Los Angeles, CA: New Leaf Press, 2000), 201.

81 As quoted in *Current Thoughts and Trends* (Jan 1995): 26.

82 Hunter, George C. *The Celtic Way of Evangelism* (Nashville, TN: Abingdon Press, 2000), 111.

83 Sweet, Leonard. *Soul Tsunami: Sink or Swim in the New Millennium Culture* (Grand Rapids, MI: Zondervan Publishing House, 1999), 391.

84 Ibid, 199.

85 Easum, Bill and Bandy, Thomas. *Growing Spiritual Redwoods* (Nashville: Abingdon Press, 1997), 51.

86 Pine, B. Joseph. *Mass Customization* (Boston: Harvard Business School Press, 1993).

87 Naisbitt, John. "Beyond the Service Economy," *John Naisbitt's Trend Letter* (15 Dec 1996), 2.

88 Pine, B. Joseph and Gilmore, James. *The Experience Economy: Work Is Theatre and Every Business A Stage* (Boston: Harvard Business School Press, 1999), 1.

89 Borgmann, Albert. *Crossing the Postmodern Divide* (Chicago: University of Chicago Press, 1992).

90 Pine and Gilmore, 96.

91 Ibid., 165.

92 Ibid, 190.

93 Ibid., 171.

94 Warren, Rick, "You Don't Have to Stay the Same" audio message, March, 2001.

95 Ferguson, David and Teresa and Thurman, Chris and Holly. *The Pursuit of Intimacy: What Being in Love was Meant to Be* (Nashville, TN: Thomas Nelson Publishers, 1993), 75-84.

96 Schwarz, Christian. *The 3 Colors of Ministry* (St. Charles, IL: Church Smart Resources, 2001), 42.

97 Ford, Paul, "Your Cell Group: The Best Place to Discover and Use Spiritual Gifts," *Cell Group Journal (Volume 10, Number 3, Summer 2001)*, 9.

98 Walker, John, quoting George Barna in *Barna: Terrorist Attacks Did Not Change Most Americans Spiritually,* www.pastors.com, 13 January 2002.

[99] Ibid.

[100] Grossman, Cathy Lynn, *A Measure of Faith,* USA Today, 24 December 2001, p. 4d.

[101] Zens, Jon, *Four Tragic Shifts in the Visible Church 180-400 A.D.,* www.geocities.com, 6 September, 2001.

[102] Breslau, Eleanor, "The Real Story of Flight 93," *Newsweek* (3 December 2001): 58.

[103] Ibid, 58.

[104] Ibid, 61.

[105] Ibid, 64.

[106] Ibid, 64.

[107] Ibid, 67.

Printed in the United States
31264LVS00002B/38

9 781591 604952